English for Baseball

Conversation, Vocabulary, Idioms & Fun

Targets in English

Visit us on the Web at

www.TargetsInEnglish.com

Find us on Facebook

Facebook.com/TargetsInEnglish

First edition, 2015.

By John Sailors

Targets in English is an imprint of Story Crest Press.

ISBN: 978-1-938688-10-2

Schools interested in using Targets in English books

can contact us at into@storycrest.com.

Find us: Facebook.com/TargetsInEnglish

www.TargetsInEnglish.com

Credits

Contents

Introduction

Baseball has been around for more than two hundred years. The sport became America's favorite pastime early on, and in the last fifty years, it has become popular around the world. Today, you can find baseball players and fans in Latin America, Asia, Europe, and elsewhere.

English for Baseball teaches the conversation, vocabulary, and grammar needed to talk about the sport in English or watch English broadcasts of the game. The book covers baseball English step by step, from the players and the field, to running and fielding, to baseball leagues. It is aimed at low-intermediate to advanced students.

Each unit introduces essential baseball vocabulary, which then appears in readings, lively conversations, funny comics, and interesting baseball facts. Language notes and explanations make understanding easy.

In addition, Unit 9 of the book teaches the 50 most-common English idioms that come from baseball, phrases used commonly in everyday English conversartion.

Finally, Unit 10 is a quick baseball dictionary that makes it easy for learners to look up words taught in the book.

English for Baseball allows learners to improve their English as well as their understanding of a sport that is loved the world over. And it teaches the language in a way that is fun and easy to remember.

For more information, visit the Targets in English website and find us on Facebook.

1. Baseball Players

Play Ball

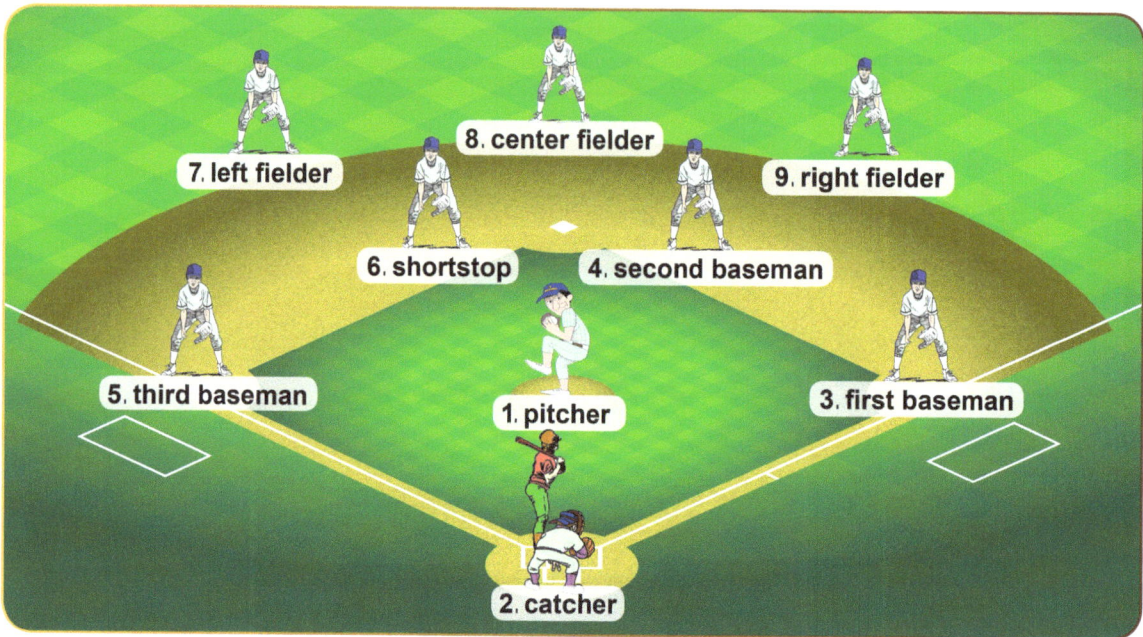

8. center fielder
7. left fielder
9. right fielder
6. shortstop
4. second baseman
5. third baseman
1. pitcher
3. first baseman
2. catcher

1. pitcher*

Tom is learning how to play pitcher.

Cy Young was a pitcher on five teams.

2. catcher*

I'm reading a book on how to play catcher.

Catchers use catcher's mitts.

3. first baseman

John is our first baseman.

Throw it to the first baseman.

4. second baseman

I'm usually the second baseman.

Jenny wants to be the second baseman.

5. third baseman

Ted is a good third baseman.

Third basemen need to have strong arms.

6. shortstop

I got to play shortstop yesterday.

Many balls are hit toward the shortstop, so he must be fast.

7. left fielder

Donny is usually our left fielder.

Who wants to be the left fielder?

8. center fielder

The center fielder caught the ball.

Paul, you're the center fielder, not the left fielder.

9. right fielder

Danny was our right fielder today.

A right fielder must be able to catch the ball while running.

10. batter*

Hank is the first batter, and Gina is the second batter.

Which batter is up to bat now?

11. umpire*

An umpire must have a good eye to make good calls.

The umpire is always right. Never argue with an umpire.

12. first-base coach*

The first base coach tells runners what to do as they near first base.

Watch the first base coach when you're running to first.

13. third-base coach*

I'll be the third-base coach today.

The third-base coach signaled Hal to run for home.

14. manager*

The manager is the head coach on a baseball team.

Our manager has put together a great team.

Arguing with the umpire.

Language Notes:

1) **pitcher:** *Pitcher, catcher,* and *batter* come from the verbs *pitch, catch,* and *bat.* See more on these words in units 4 and 5.

2) **umpire:** The main umpire is the *home plate umpire.* A game may also have a *field umpire.* People sometimes call umpires "blue" because of the color of the uniforms they usually wear.

3) **manager:** Head coaches in base-ball are called managers. Other coaches in the game include:

- assistant coach
- first-base coach
- third-base coach
- pitching coach
- hitting coach
- bench coach
- trainers

Baseball's Pitch Catches On

George Gibson, catcher, Pittsburgh Pirates, 1908 (left); Herb Pennock, pitcher, Philadelphia A's, 1914 (right).

Catcher: Catchers work harder than any player on a team. They often play the whole game, **crouching** behind batters and going after every pitch.

Catchers can see the whole field, so they can **lead** their team in **defensive** play.* They also tell pitchers which pitches to throw, by using secret **hand signals**.

Because of their understanding of the game, many catchers make excellent managers.

Pitcher: The pitcher is the most important part of a team's **defense** and many have **amazing** arms.*

Children age 10 and younger can pitch as fast as 40 miles per hour (64 kilometers per hour).

Some professional pitchers throw at speeds of more than 100 miles per hour (161 kilometers). They also learn special pitches such as **fastballs** and **curveballs** that are much harder for batters to hit.*

Baseball Facts

George Gibson was a baseball player from Canada who joined the Pittsburgh Pirates in 1905. He played catcher for the Pirates when they won the 1909 World Series against the Detroit Tigers. He later became manager of the Pirates and also the Chicago Cubs.

George Gibson, 1909.

Dictionary

1. **crouch,** *v.*, to bend your knees so you are closer to the ground.

   The catcher crouches behind the batter to catch pitches.

2. **lead,** *v.*, to control people, to tell them what to do.

   Our manager leads our team well.

3. **defensive,** *adj.*, on defense, trying to stop a team from scoring.*

   George is a good defensive player.

4. **hand signal,** *n. phr.*, a secret gesture with your hand to tell someone something.

   The pitcher waited for the catcher's hand signal.

5. **defense,** *n.*, a team when it is on the field, trying to stop the other team from scoring.*

   Our team plays great on defense, but poorly on offense.

Catcher and umpire crouching behind plate.

6. **amazing,** *adj.*, fantastic, hard to believe.*

   Mike is an amazing pitcher.

7. **fastball,** *n.*, a pitch that is thrown as fast as possible, to make it difficult to hit. See more in Unit 4.*

   Randy has a great fastball.

8. **curveball,** *n.*, a pitch that curves as it flies to the plate, making it more difficult to hit. See more in Unit 4.*

   Hank threw a curveball on the last pitch, not a fastball.

Language Notes

1) **defense/defensive:** Many sports have an *offense* (players trying to score points) and a *defense* (players trying to stop scoring). These are American spellings. In British English, a C is used instead of an S: *defence, offence.*

2) **amazing:** The verb is *to amaze.* The pitcher amazes me. He is *amazing.* I was *amazed* when I watched him pitch.

3) **fastball & curveball:** When two-word nouns become very common, they are often spelled as one word. Sometimes, people spell them differently: (1) curveball / curve ball (2) knuckleball / knuckle ball. *Learn more about pitches in Unit 4.*

4) **catch on:** The phrasal verb *catch on* (in the reading's title) means "to become popular," as in *Baseball caught on quickly* .

The Easiest Job in Baseball

Baseball Comics

While you guys are out there running and jumping and getting hit by the ball ...

Ed wants to join his high school baseball team, but he wants to play an easy position. Here, Joe, the coach, is giving him advice.

Joe: So what **position** do you want to play? Pitcher?

Ed: I can't play pitcher! I've never played baseball before.

Joe: Ah yes! Pitchers have to have **experience**.* And they have to be able to pitch fast.

Ed: How about catcher? Is it hard to play catcher?*

Joe: It's very hard. Catchers work harder than anyone.* And they often play the whole game.

Ed: How about a first baseman? What does a first baseman have to do?

Joe: First basemen must be able to catch throws from every other player, and keep their foot on the base.

Ed: Do first basemen have to be fast?

Joe: No, but it helps if they're tall. Also, sometimes **left-handed** players make the best first basemen.

Ed: I can't catch very well, and I'm not tall. How about second base or shortstop?

Joe: Second basemen and short- stops have to be very fast and have a strong arm.

Ed: I'm not that fast. How about third basemen? Does a third baseman have to be fast?

Joe: No, but a good third baseman has to catch well and throw far—all the way to first base.

Ed: That sounds hard. How about the outfielders? Can I be a right fielder, a center fielder, or a left fielder? Are those easy jobs?

Joe: No, but they can be good positions for **beginners**.

Ed: So the outfielders have the easiest jobs on a baseball team?

Joe: No, of course not.

Ed: Then who has the easiest job?

Joe: I do. While you guys run around, I just relax and drink lemonade.

Dictionary

1. **position,** *n.*, a player's job, such as a pitcher or a catcher.

   Catchers have the most difficult position.

2. **experience,** *n.*, skill in a job or sport because you have done or played it before.*

   Jim has a lot of experience as a baseball manager.

4. **left-handed,** *adj.*, used to using your left hand. The opposite is *right-handed*.

   Are you right-handed or left-handed? I'm right-handed.

The player with the hardest job.

4. **beginner,** *n.*, someone who has just started doing something.

   Jake is a beginner at baseball.

5. **outfielder,** *n.*, a player who plays outside the bases, in the outfield. See more in unit 2.

   Since Jake was a beginner, he started as an outfielder.

Language Notes

1) **experience:** *Experience* here is an uncountable noun, as in *much experience* or *a little experience. I have experience at baseball. I have experience pitching.*

2) **hard:** As an adjective, *hard* means "difficult," as in *Playing baseball is hard*. As an adverb, it means "to do something with a lot of effort," as in *work hard*.

2. The Baseball Field

Play Ball

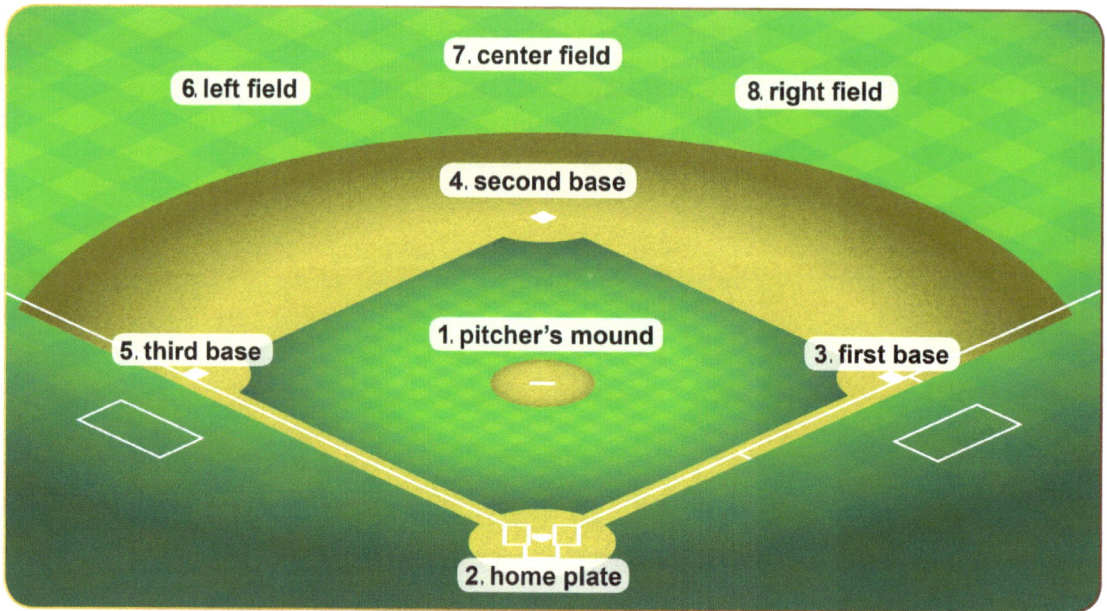

7. center field
6. left field
8. right field
4. second base
1. pitcher's mound
5. third base
3. first base
2. home plate

1. **pitcher's mound,** *n. phr.*, a small hill where a pitcher throws from.

   Hey, Sam, take the mound (= go out and pitch).*

2. **home plate,** *n.*, the spot where a batter bats.

   Kate pitched the ball right over home plate.

3. **first base,** *n.*, the first spot a runner must reach.

   I threw the ball to first base before the runner got there.

4. **second base,** *n.*, the second spot a runner must reach.

   Jimmy plays second base; he's the second baseman.

5. **third base,** *n.*, the third spot a runner must reach.

   When the outfielder dropped the ball, Mike made it to third (base).*

6. **left field,** *n.*, the area beyond the bases and to the batter's left.

   Jake is in left field today. He's playing left field.

7. **center field,** *n.*, the area beyond the bases and straight ahead.

   Kyle is the center fielder. He's playing center field.

8. **right field,** *n.*, the area beyond the bases and to the batter's right.

   Timmy caught two fly balls in right field today.

9. outfield
10. infield
11. foul line
11. foul line
12. coach's box
12. coach's box
13. on-deck circle
13. on-deck circle
14. batter's box
15. catcher's box

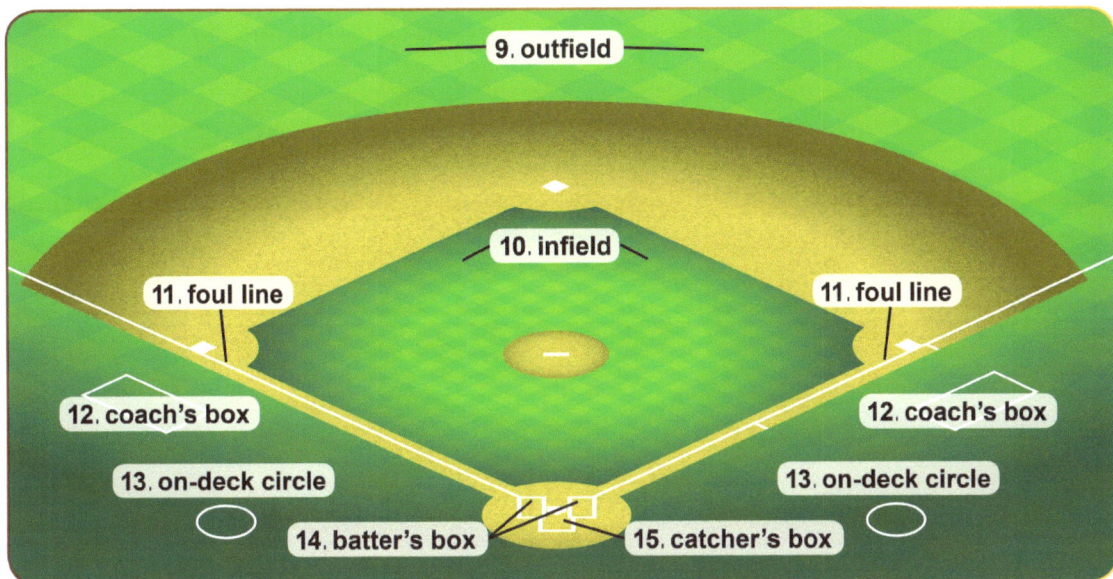

9. **outfield (outfielder),** *n.*, the part of the field beyond the bases.

Vick always hits into the outfield.

10. **infield (infielder),** *n.*, the part of the field within the bases.

The shortstop plays in the infield.

11. **foul line,** *n.*, lines between home and first base and home and third.*

The ball rolled outside the foul line.

12. **coach's box,** *n. phr.*, a box next to first and third for base coaches.

Base coaches stand in the coaches' boxes to help batters.

13. **on-deck circle,** *n. phr.*, a circle where the next batter up waits.*

Wait in the on-deck circle to bat.

14. **batter's box,** *n. phr.*, a box where batters stand to bat. There are boxes for left-handed and right-handed batters.

Step out of the batter's box and rest between pitches.

15. **catcher's box,** *n. phr.*, an area behind home plate where a catcher crouches to play.

The catcher crouches behind home plate, in the catcher's box. The umpire stands behind him.

Language Notes:

1) **take the mound:** This means "go out and pitch."

2) **base:** Often just the *number* is used: *There's a runner on first.*

3) **foul line:** Foul balls are hit outside the foul lines.

4) **on deck:** The player who is next in line to bat.

Building the Perfect Field

Fenway Park, Boston, Massachusetts, 1913.

The baseball **diamond** is **designed** to make the sport as **competitive** as possible.* In professional baseball, the bases are 90 feet (27.4 meters) apart, a distance that was set in the 1840s.

Over the years, players found that if the bases were farther apart, the game would be too hard for the offense. If they were closer, it would be too hard for the defense.

In early baseball, pitchers were only 45 feet from home plate, and they threw **underhand**, as they do today in **softball**.*

In 1881, pitchers were moved back 5 feet, to 50 feet (15.2 meters), and in 1884, **overhand** pitching was allowed. Today the pitcher is 60.5 feet (18.4 meters) away from the batter.

There are **exact measurements** for every part of the field but one: the outfield. The distance from home plate to the fence can be from 300 feet (91.4 meters) to 435 feet (132.6 meters).

Of course, if the outfield is larger, it is harder to hit the ball over the fence. The heights of the fences, or walls, are different in various ballparks, too.

Baseball Facts

Fenway Park, in Boston, has been home to the Boston Red Sox since it opened in 1912. It is the oldest stadium still used in Major League Baseball, after several renovations over the years.

Image left, the outside of Fenway Park, 1914.

Dictionary

1. **diamond,** *n.*, a square with one corner pointing up; the main part of a baseball field.

   These are the measurements for a baseball diamond.

2. **design,** *v.*, to plan something with a certain goal.

   They designed the ballpark to make it hold lots of fans.

3. **competitive,** *adj.*, (1) hard to win; (2) wanting very much to win.*

   Baseball is a very competitive sport. Players try hard to win.

4. **underhand,** *adv./adj.*, to throw a ball with your hand from low to high.

   Show me how to pitch underhand.

5. **softball,** *n.*, a form of baseball that uses a larger and softer ball.*

   Rita is going to join her company's softball team.

Overhand and underhand throws.

6. **overhand,** *adv./adj.*, to throw a ball above your shoulder.

   Jill's overhand pitch is very good.

7. **exact,** *adj.*, correct in every way.

   All the distances on the baseball field must be exact.

8. **measurement,** *n.*, a number that shows something's size, after measuring it.

   Here are the measurements for the baseball field.

Language Notes

1) **competitive:** The verb is *compete*, as in *The teams compete to see which is the best.* The noun is *competition*, as in *We had a batting competition to see who could hit the most pitches.*

2) **softball:** Softball is a popular sport in schools and universities, as well as for adults who are not professional players. Many companies have softball teams.

Also in the Park

- **dugout:** a place where players sit when not playing.

- **bullpen:** a place where pitchers can warm up.

- **bleachers:** outdoor benches where people sit to watch games. These are common at school fields.

- **snackbar:** a place that sells foods and drinks. For young players and many people watching, this is their favorite part of a ballpark.

Who's the Manager?

Baseball Comics

LET ME MAKE **ONE** CHANGE IN THE LINEUP.

Jim is the manager of a neighborhood baseball team. He is talking to Ben, an **assistant coach**.*

Jim: I've made some changes in the **roster**, Ben.*

Ben: Really? What changes?

Jim: Well, to begin with, Joey is going to play first.

Ben: What?! Joey's our second baseman. If Joey plays first, who's on second?

Jim: I put Jack on second.

Ben: Jack?! He's our third baseman. Who's on third, then?

Jim: Sammy is going to play third base today.

Ben: Well, Sammy is a good third baseman, but he's our star shortstop. Who'll play shortstop?

Jim: Timothy's going to play short-stop today.

Ben: Timothy can't play shortstop! He isn't a good infielder. That's why we put him in the outfield.

Jim: I know, but I want to give him a **chance**.* Oh, and Harold's playing catcher today.

Ben: Harold play catcher? He drops the ball when you hand it to him!

Jim: And Frank's pitching.

Ben: Are you kidding? Hank can't throw straight. He has a **glass arm**.

Jim: Well, I want to give him a chance, too.

Ben: If these are our **starters**, then we're going to lose today.

Jim: Everyone gets a chance.

Ben: Then can I make one change? There's one more person who needs a chance.

Jim: Sure, everyone gets a chance. Who is it?

Ben: Me. Let *me* be the manager and make the roster!

Jim: Wait a minute!

Dictionary

1. **assistant coach,** *n. phr.*, a coach who helps a manager.*

   Our manager is sick, so the assistant coach is the boss today.

2. **roster,** *n.*, a list showing what players play what positions.*

   We're going to have a new player on our roster next month.

3. **chance,** *n.*, a time to try something; an opportunity.*

   Everyone will get a chance to bat.

Hank had a glass arm today.

4. **glass arm,** *n. phr.*, an arm that tires and cannot throw well.

   Kyle is a great batter, but he has a glass arm.

5. **starter,** *n.*, a player who starts a game.

   Dennis will be a starter tomorrow.

Language Notes

1) **assistant:** Many jobs have assistants: assistant coach, assistant teacher, assistant manager. The verb *assist* means "to help." In baseball, players get an *assist (n.)* on their record if they help put a runner out.

2) **roster:** In Major League Baseball, teams have a main, 25-man roster and a 40-man roster.

3) **chance:** In youth sports, teams talk about giving all players a *chance* to play, even if they are not the best.

3. Baseball Equipment

Play Ball

1. baseball

2. bat

3. baseball hat

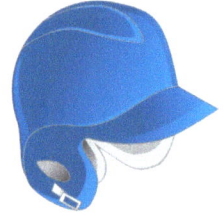

4. batting helmet

5. baseball glove

6. catcher's mitt

7. batting gloves

8. cleats

1. baseball*

All youth baseball games must use the correct baseballs.

2. bat

Never throw the bat after you hit the ball. Drop it before you run.

3. baseball hat

Wear a baseball hat to keep the sun out of your eyes.

4. batting helmet

Batting helmets are essential for batters' safety.

5. glove / fielding glove*

Tim is left-handed, so he wears a glove on his right hand.

6. catcher's mitt

A catcher's mitt is thick to protect the catcher's hand.

7. batting gloves

Batting gloves protect batters' hands.

8. cleats*

Getting stepped on by cleats really hurts!

9. baseball uniform

For uniforms this year we have red shirts and striped pants.

10. shirt/jersey

Our team has our names on our jerseys.

9. baseball uniform
10. jersey
11. pants
12. socks

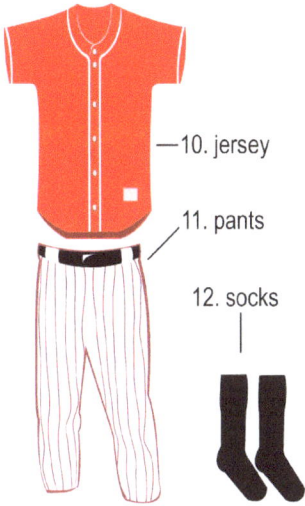

13. catcher's gear
14. catcher's helmet
15. chest protector
16. leg guards

17. undershirt
18. belt

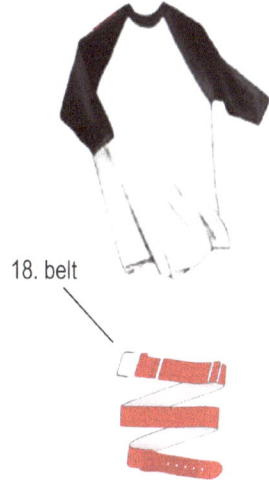

11. baseball pants

Our baseball pants have a stripe on the leg.

12. socks

Be sure to wear red socks with your uniform.

13. catcher's gear

Catcher's equipment protects you when you get hit by the ball.

14. catcher's helmet

Many catchers throw their helmets off when they need to see better.

15. chest protector

Make sure the chest protector is on tight.

16. leg guards

Leg guards protect a catcher's knees and lower legs.

17. undershirt

Wearing an undershirt will help you stay warm.

18. belt

All players on our team wear red belts and red socks.

Language Notes:

1) **baseball:** Baseball uses *hardballs*; the game softball uses *softballs*.

2) **gloves:** Players use *fielding gloves*, or just *gloves,* and *catcher's mitts,* which have the fingers together.

3) **cleats:** The shoes and the spikes on the bottom are called cleats.

4) **pairs:** For gloves, cleats, pants, socks, and leg guards, use *pair*, as in *pair of socks, two pairs of socks*.

Who Needs Baseball Gear?

The Atlantics of Brooklyn baseball club, c. 1865. The Atlantics were a leading team in the 1860s.

In early baseball, players used little **gear**—just a ball and a bat. Tough players felt they didn't need equipment, and many **preferred** to get **beaned** rather than wear a glove or a helmet. If you've ever been hit by a baseball, you know just how serious these players were.

The ball: In the mid-1800s, players often made balls themselves, of different sizes and weights. They were made of **yarn** or string and covered with a piece of **leather**.

In 1871, the National Association of Baseball Players began making **rules** on equipment, and the ball has changed little since. Today's baseballs are 9 inches in **circumference** and weigh 5 ounces.

The bat: The first bats were heavier and thicker and could be any length the batter wanted.* At one time, they were also flat on one side. In the 1880s, new rules required round bats with a standard size and weight. Today, MLB bats are 2.75 inches in **diameter** at the thickest part, and no more than 42 inches in length.*

The glove: For years, players did not wear gloves. They preferred to be tough and play without. But in the 1870s, many got smart and used simple gloves to **pad** their hands. The first gloves were made of several layers of leather and had no fingers.

Again it was in the 1870s that **standards** were set, and gloves have been part of the game since.

Dictionary

1. **gear**, *n.*, tools. For baseball, both *gear* and *equipment* are used.

   Remember to bring your baseball gear to the game.

2. **prefer**, *v.*, to like something better, to want it more than another.

   Leslie prefers watching baseball to football.

3. **bean**, *v.*, to hit on the head, especially a baseball.

   Hank got beaned by a batted ball the last time he played pitcher.

4. **yarn**, *n.*, thread used for knitting, as in knitting a sweater.

   Some early baseballs were made with yarn.

5. **leather**, *n.*, animal skin used for shoes, etc. Also an adjective.

   Most baseball gloves are made of leather.

6. **rule**, *n.*, an instruction saying what you can or cannot do.

   You must always follow the rules; never break the rules.

7. **circumference**, *n.*, the distance around a round object or a circle.

   The circumference of a baseball is 9 inches.

8. **diameter**, *n.*, the distance through the center of a round object or circle.

   The diameter of a baseball bat is 2.75 inches.

9. **pad**, *v.*, to add soft material, for protection. Also a noun: *pad, padding*.

   Early baseball gloves were padded with just leather.

10. **standard**, *n.*, measurements everyone must follow. Also and adjective.

    The baseball league sets standards for the size and weight of balls.

Baseball Facts

In the 1970s the Oakland A's tried to introduce orange baseballs.* A's owner Charlie O. Finley thought they would be easier to see. But the balls were not a hit with players, so he struck out with the idea.* Among other of Finley's ideas was to give players $300 bonuses for growing moustaches during championships.

Language Notes

1) **long/length:** *adj./n.* Also: wide/width; high/height; deep/depth.

2) **Athletics:** The Athletics are often called just the A's.

3) **hit:** *Hit,* here, means "very popular," as in *The movie was a hit*.

4) **strike out:** Means "to fail." See unit 9 on baseball idioms.

What Makes Gear a Hit?

Baseball Comics

Panel 1: I don't think Pete's going to play today. He got beaned yesterday.

Panel 2: Both as batter **and** pitcher.

Panel 3: Then he got stepped on. So I don't think...

Panel 4: I'm ready to play, Coach. I just needed the right equipment!

Fred, the manager of a youth baseball team, is talking to Kate, the team's catcher. Kate missed **practice** *yesterday, and she is now learning what happened.*

Fred: Pete may not play in the game today.

Kate: Why not? He's our best batter. We need him.

Fred: He got hurt a couple times in practice yesterday.

Kate: Really? I wasn't there. What happened?

Fred: He got beaned while batting.

Kate: Well, players get hit by baseballs a lot. They have to **walk it off**.*

Fred: Yeah, but Pete got hit three times.

Kate: Three times? That's hard to walk off.

Fred: Right! And later, he **tripped over** the **bag** on first base and fell on his head.*

Kate: Oh no! Poor Pete.

Fred: And while he was on the ground, the first baseman **stepped on** Pete's hand.

Kate: Ouch. That's terrible. With cleats?

Fred: Yes. And that's not all. Later, another player threw the bat and it hit Pete in the stomach.

Kate: Oh no. Baseball isn't a **contact** sport!*

Fred: Yeah, and later, Pete was on the ground next to home plate, and the catcher stepped on him.

Kate: Was the catcher wearing catcher's gear?

Fred: Yeah. So Pete may not come today. He may be too scared.

(Pete walks up from behind.)

Pete: Hey, Coach. No, I'm not scared.

Fred: Hey, you can't wear football pads in a baseball game!

Dictionary

1. **practice,** *n.*, a time when sports teams try to improve. Also a verb.

   We have baseball practice after school every day.

2. **walk off,** *phrasal verb*, to walk around to recover from an illness.*

   When Jenny got beaned, the coach told her to walk it off.

3. **trip over,** *phrasal verb*, to fall because your foot hits something.*

   Pete tripped over the bat.

4. **bag,** *n.*, the square white marker on first, second, and third bases.

   Keep your foot on the bag.

5. **step on,** *phrasal verb*, to put your foot onto something.

   Be careful; don't step on your teammates.

6. **contact,** *n.*, the touching of other people. Used here as an adjective.*

   American football and rugby are contact sports.

Language Notes

1) **walk off:** In youth sports, when players are hurt but not seriously, a coach or a parent will often them to "walk it off."

2) **trip:** *Trip* is a transitive verb (Joe tripped me and I fell) and an intransitive verb (I tripped and fell). Add *over* to say what the foot hit, as in *I tripped over the cat*.

3) **contact:** A contact sport is one where players have contact with each other, such as American football and rugby. In contact sports, players are more likely to get hurt.

4. Pitching & Catching

Pitching Grips

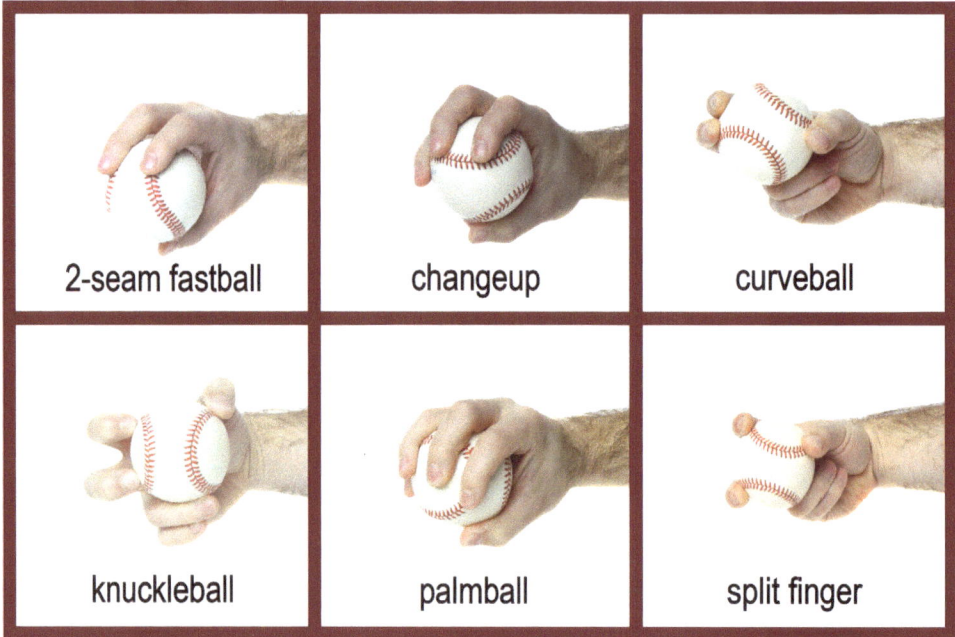

2-seam fastball	changeup	curveball
knuckleball	palmball	split finger

1. **fastball,** *n.*, a pitch thrown as fast as the pitcher can.

   Jim's fastball is hard to hit. He has a great fastball.

2. **breaking ball,** *n. phr.*, a pitch where the ball moves to the side or down.

   Jim's breaking ball usually fools batters.

3. **curveball,** *n.*, a pitch thrown to make the ball spin and fall downward.

   Their pitcher surprised me with a curveball.

4. **changeup,** *n.*, a pitch that's slower, to fool the batter. Also: *slowball*.

   Lester is practicing changeups.

5. **knuckleball,** *n.*, a pitch with no spin; so its path is hard to predict.

   I'll teach you how to throw a knuckleball.

6. **slider,** *n.*, a pitch that flies to the side and down.

   Frank has been having trouble hitting sliders.

7. **spitball,** *n.*, a pitch when the ball has been spit on to change how it flies.

   Hank got into trouble for throwing spitballs. They're against the rules.

8. **call the game,** *v. phr.*, to choose what pitches are thrown.*

   Our coach will call the game.

strike zone

hand signal

9. **strike zone,** *n.*, a space above home plate and between a batter's knees and chest.*

The pitch was inside the strike zone, so it was a strike.

10. **strike,** *n.*, a pitch inside the strike zone that is not hit. Also, a pitch outside that is swung at but not hit.

Our pitcher threw almost all strikes today.

11. **ball,** *n.*, a pitch outside the strike zone that is not swung at.

OK, you have two balls and one strike.

12. **signal,** *n.*, to use a hand gesture to communicate. Also a verb.

The catcher uses hand signals to tell the pitcher which pitch to throw.

13. **framing,** *n.*, (catchers) holding their mitt inside the strike zone, to make pitches look like strikes.

Sam's learning to frame pitches, so umpires will call more strikes.

14. **blocking,** *n.*, (catchers) using their body to stop pitches that hit the ground, or are "in the dirt."*

If the ball is in the dirt, don't try to catch it; block the pitch instead.

Language Notes:

1) **call the game:** Often, catchers call the game, though managers sometimes make calls. The catcher is considered a captain on the field.

2) **strike zone:** The strike zone is from the middle of the torso to the knees. Umpires may have different ideas of how big a strike zone is, especially with batters of different sizes. An umpire may be said to "have a large/small strike zone."

3) **in the dirt:** If a pitch hits the ground, it is often said to be "in the dirt."

4) **pitches:** Other names for pitches include:

- **fastballs:** cutter, four-seam, two-seam, sinker.
- **breaking balls:** curveball, knuckle curve, screwball, slider.
- **changeups:** circle changeup, forkball, palmball.

Baseball Makes a Pitch

Cy Young, Boston, 1908.

Pitching is **hard** on the arm, and several pitchers are often needed for a game. So teams have a *bullpen*—a group of players who can pitch when needed.* As the starting pitcher **tires out**, **relief pitchers** are **put in**.* Teams may also have a **closer**, a pitcher who is hot at the end of a game.

Most pitchers try to learn at least two or three kinds of pitches. Some can throw up to six. By throwing different pitches, they make it much harder for batters to hit the ball.

Many pitchers throw a mix of fastballs and changeups. A changeup looks like a fastball, but arrives at a much-slower speed. Pro pitchers throw fastballs up to 100 miles (160 kilometers) per hour. Their changeups may travel at only 75 to 85 miles per hour (120–129 kilometers)—a difference that fools batters.

Young, Boston, 1902.

One of the greatest pitchers ever was Cy Young, who played from 1890 to 1911 and still **holds** several MLB records.* During his 21 years in baseball, he had 511 wins, which is still the most ever.

Young also still holds records for the most innings pitched (7,356) and the most games he started in (815). A year after his death, the Cy Young Award was created to honor the best pitchers of each season.

Dictionary

1. **hard,** *adj.*, able to cause damage to; destructive to.

   The way catchers crouch can be hard on their knees.

2. **bullpen,** *n.*, (1) a place at a field where pitchers warm up. Also called *the pen*. (2) the relief pitchers on a baseball team.*

   Our bullpen failed us in yesterday's game; no one pitched well.

3. **tire out,** *phrasal verb*, to become weak or tired after work or exercise; to make weak or tired.

   New players often tire out easily and quickly.

4. **relief pitcher,** *n. phr.*, a pitcher who comes in after a starting pitcher.*

   Ned was a starting pitcher last year, but this year, he's a relief pitcher.

5. **put in,** *phrasal verb*, to send a player into a game to play. The opposite is *take out*.

   The coach took Ed out of the game and put Paul in to replace him.

6. **closer,** *n.*, a relief pitcher who specializes in getting the final outs in a game. This often is a team's best relief pitcher.*

   With a two-run lead, they're putting in their closer.

7. **hold,** *v.*, to have and/or maintain a record.*

   For a long time, Babe Ruth held the record for the most home runs.

Language Notes

1) **bullpen:** Pitchers can warm up (get ready to play) by throwing practice pitches in the bullpen, an area where they will not be hit by the ball during a game.

2) **relief:** Someone who takes another person's place at a job, as in *I can't go home until my relief arrives*.

3) **record:** Common verbs used with record are *set, break,* and *hold* (a record), as in *I set a new record. I broke the old record and now I hold the record*.

4) **make a pitch:** The idiom in the title means "to speak to promote something." If you make a pitch, you try to convince people of something.

The Hardest Pitch to Hit?

Baseball Comics

Sam the Slugger can hit the fastball, the slowball, the curveball, the spitball....

There's only one pitch he can't hit...

It's called just "**the ball.**"

Kyle, the catcher on a high school baseball team, walks to the mound to talk to Joe, the pitcher. Joe looks scared.

Kyle: The next batter is Sam Smith. They call him Sam the **Slugger**.*

Joe: I know. He's the best batter in the **state**.*

Kyle: He can hit any pitch. So I want you to—

Joe: I'll throw a fastball! I'll bet he can't hit my fastball.

Kyle: Your fastball isn't fast enough for Sam the Slugger.

Joe: Really? Then I'll throw a changeup and **fool** him. He'll be expecting a fastball.

Kyle: Sam can hit high, low, fast and slow, so that won't work.

Joe: OK, how about this? I'll throw my **secret** curveball.

Kyle: We keep your curveball a secret because it doesn't work.

Joe: Oh, well, then how about a good ol' slider?

Kyle: Your sliders always *slide* along the ground—in the dirt.

Joe: Oh, that's true. Hey, I could try a spitball. Spitballs can be really hard to hit!

Kyle: Spitballs are **against** the rules, and they're really **gross** if you're the catcher.

Joe: So what should I throw? Is there any pitch that Sam the Slugger can't hit?

Kyle: There is *one* pitch he can't hit, the pitch that no batter can.

Joe: What's that?

Kyle: The ball—the "we're going to walk you" pitch. Throw him four.

Dictionary

1. **slugger,** *n.*, a good batter in base-ball, who can hit very hard.*

   That team has some real sluggers.

2. **state,** *n.*, one of the fifty states in the U.S.*

   Our team won the state champion-ship last year.

3. **fool,** *v.*, to make someone believe something that is not true.

   He fooled me with a fastball.

4. **secret,** *adj.*, something other people don't know. Also a noun.

   Kenny has a secret pitch that can fool batters.

Sing: "We will, we will, WALK you."

5. **against (rules),** *prep.*, not allowed, according to the rules.

   There's a rule against spitballs. They're against the rules.

6. **gross,** *adj.*, disgusting.

   The dugout has not been cleaned all year; it is really gross.

Language Notes

1) **slugger:** The verb *to slug* means "to hit hard." The word has been used both for baseball players and boxers who hit hard.

2) **state:** In youth and high school sports, teams may compete for state championships.

Baseball Facts

Batters who are likely to get big hits are often walked. The batter with the most *intentional walks* (intentional bases on balls, or IBBs) during his MLB career is Barry Bonds, who has 688 IBBs. Baseball legend Hank Aaron follows with 293. IBBs were first tracked in 1955.

5. Batting

At the Plate

1. at bat	2. on deck	3. swing
4. hit	5. miss	6. bunt

1. **at-bat,** *n.,* a turn trying to hit the ball. The plural is *at-bats.**

   Barry had three at-bats today, and he got a hit with each.

2. **on deck,** *adj. phr.,* next in line to bat.

   Smith is batting, and Sanchez is on deck.

3. **swing,** *v.,* to move the bat to try and hit the ball. Also a noun.

   Swing a few times before entering the batter's box. Take a few swings.

4. **hit,** *v.,* to strike a ball with a bat. Also a noun.

   Jim hasn't been able to hit the ball all day. He had no hits.

5. **miss,** *v.,* to swing but not hit a ball; to fail to hit something.

   That pitcher's curveballs are easy to miss.

6. **bunt,** *v.,* to hold the bat out and let a pitch hit it, usually as a surprise.*

   If you bunt, you'll help advance a runner.

7. **foul,** *n./adj.,* a hit ball that goes outside the foul line. Also: *foul ball.*

   Fred hit four foul balls before getting on base.

8. **fair,** *adj.,* (a hit ball) inside the foul line. Also: *fair ball (n. phr.).*

   The ball was fair! It was inside the foul line. Run to first!

9. **single,** *n.,* a hit that allows the batter to run to first base.

Ralph hit two singles today.

10. **double,** *n.,* a hit that allows the batter to run to second base.

Sanchez is going to get a double out of that hit.

11. **triple,** *n.,* a hit that allows the batter to run to third base.

Jake hit a triple and nearly got to home plate.

12. **run**, *n.,* a point scored in baseball. The plural is *runs.*

We scored seven runs today.

13. **home run,** *n.,* a hit that allows a batter to run all three bases and back to home plate.

Eric hit two home runs today. We call Eric the Home Run King.

14. **grand slam,** *n.,* a home run when all three bases have runners.

A grand slam now would give us four runs and we'd win.

15. **drive in,** *phrasal verb,* to hit the ball and another player scores a run.

Try to drive in the runner on third.

16. **RBI,** *n.,* runs batted in. The plural is *RBIs.*

Carl had four RBIs today.

17. **count,** *n.,* the number of balls and strikes a batter has.*

What's the count? The count is three and two.

18. **strike out,** *phrasal verb,* to be out on three strikes. Noun: *strikeout.*

Ben rarely strikes out, but he struck out today. It was a rare strikeout.

19. **walk,** *n.,* a free walk to first base because the pitcher throws four balls. Also a verb.

We got a lot of walks in today's game.

20. **line drive,** *n.,* a hit ball that goes straight, close to the ground.

Victor hit a line drive to left field and ran to first.

Language Notes:

1) **at-bat:** As a noun, the term is spelled either with a hyphen or as two words: at-bat, at bat(s).

2) **bunt:** When players bunt, it is often a sacrifice bunt—they may not reach first base, but will help other players advance.

3) **full count:** If a batter has three balls and two strikes, it is called a *full count*. Umpire signals above.

Batting to New Heights

Babe Ruth, Boston Red Sox, 1919.

Batting in baseball is one of the most difficult **feats** in sports. Batters use a thin bat to try to hit a small ball that is traveling fast—at up to 100 miles per hour.

Baseball players build *batting averages* from game to game, measuring their **performance** as batters. You **calculate** a batting average by dividing the number of hits by the total number of at-bats.

Players who have a batting average of .300 (pronounced "three hundred") or better are considered strong hitters. A batting average of .400 ("four hundred") for a whole season is nearly impossible.*

The last player to **maintain** a .400 season average was Ted Williams in 1941. Williams is also one of only two players ever to win two Triple Crowns.

A player earns a Triple Crown by leading the league in batting average, home runs, and RBIs over a season.*

Williams left baseball twice, first to fight in World War II and then in the Korean War. After returning the last time, he was still batting at his best. He was the American League batting champion for the fifth and sixth times in 1957 and 1958.*

One of the greatest batters (and baseball players) ever was Babe Ruth. During his 22-year **career**, from 1914 to 1935, Ruth set records for the most home runs (714) and the most RBIs (2,213).* Babe Ruth's career batting average was a **spectacular** .342.

Dictionary

1. **feat,** *n.*, an achievement; something that is difficult to do.

   Maintaining a batting average of three fifty (.350) is a rare feat.

2. **performance,** *n.*, how one does at something such as a sport. The verb is *to perform*.

   Smith's performance on the field yesterday was fantastic. Let's see how he performs today.

3. **calculate,** *v.*, to count; to find a number. The noun is *calculation*.

   Ben calculates he will throw about five hundred pitches this year.

4. **maintain,** *v.*, to keep something; to keep something at a certain level.

   Ned maintained a batting average of two fifty (.250).

5. **career,** *n.*, your job or profession over a period of time.*

   Babe Ruth set many records during his career.

6. **spectacular,** *adj.*, amazing; amazing to watch.

   Bob had a spectacular season this year.

Baseball Facts

Babe Ruth began his baseball career as a star pitcher for the Red Sox. He later found far greater fame as a slugging outfielder for the Yankees and

Babe Ruth, with the Yankees, 1921.

went on to became one of the greatest American sports heroes.

Language Notes

1) **Triple Crown:** There is also a pitching Triple Crown, for pitchers leading a league in wins, strikeouts, and earned run average (ERA).

2) **season:** A season is the period of time in which a league plays each year. In Major League Baseball, the season usually goes from April through September. The postseason then is in October.

3) **career:** Often, one's *career* is one's lifetime work, as in *She retired after a twenty-year career in business*. For professional athletes, the term refers to their time playing a sport, as in *Babe Ruth's 22-year career*.

4) **champion:** Champions are winners, as in *MLB champions,* or the best at something, such as *batting champion* or *pitching champion*.

Comparing Hits and Runs

Baseball Comics

Today, I hit a single, two triples, and a homer.

Well, at bat today, I hit a tree, an umpire, and an angry little bird.

*Ian and Pat are very competitive. They play on different baseball teams, and they both had games today. Now they are **comparing** how they played.*

Ian: I played well today. I had four at-bats, and I got four hits.

Pat: Really? I didn't get any hits.

Ian: Ha-ha!

Pat: I can't believe you got four hits! Were they good hits?

Ian: Yeah. I hit two doubles and two triples.

Pat: You're becoming a real slugger. How many runs did you get?

Ian: Oh . . . I didn't get any runs. I was **left on base** every time.

Pat: That's impossible.

Ian: No. My teammates kept striking out.* They **let me down**.

Pat: Did you get any RBIs?

Ian: Nope. I was usually the only player on base.

Pat: Wow! Four hits and no runs. Ha-ha!

Ian: At least I **beat** you.*

Pat: No, you didn't.

Ian: But you didn't get any hits.

Pat: Right, but I had four at-bats and four intentional walks.

Ian: They walked you four times?

Pat: Yeah, and I was number three in the lineup, with Pete batting **cleanup**.*

Ian: Pete was batting after you? Pete's a strong batter.

Pat: Yeah, and he had a good day. He hit a home run every time, so I scored four runs.

Ian: I guess runs are better than hits!

Dictionary

1. **compare,** *v.*, to look at two things to see how they are similar, different, or better.

   Compare these two bats and see which one you like better.

2. **leave on base,** *v. phr.*, to still be on base after three outs, and therefore unable to score.

   Two men were left on base when I struck out.

3. **let down,** *phrasal verb*, to fail to support someone; to disappoint.

   We know our coach will always help. He never lets us down.

4. **beat,** *v.*, to win.*

   When our pitcher is hot, we beat other teams easily.

5. **cleanup,** *adv.*, fourth in the batting order. Also an adjective.*

   You want your best hitter to bat cleanup and drive runs in.

Language Notes

1) **teammate:** A *mate* is a friend. The word by itself is more common in British and Australian English. But in American English it is often used with other words: teammate, classmate, roommate, etc.

2) **beat:** This is one of many informal terms meaning "to win" or "to win over someone." Many of these terms are colorful: kill, squash, destroy, stomp, wipe out, etc.

3) **cleanup:** Cleanup hitters are usually teams' strongest batters, and players most likely to reach a base then bat before them, so they can "clean up" (drive in runs).

6. Running and Fielding

Play Ball

In the Field

1. grounder
2. pop fly
3. take a lead
4. slide
5. dive
6. tag out

1. **grounder,** *n.*, a batted ball that hits the ground and bounces.

   Ryan hit a grounder between second and third.

2. **pop fly,** *n.*, a ball hit high in the air. Also called a *fly ball*.

   The coach told the kids to practice catching pop flies.

3. **take a lead,** *v. phr.*, to step off a base before a pitch, moving toward the next base.*

   Always take a lead off the base.

4. **slide,** *v.*, to fall back onto the ground while running, to try to get a foot on base.*

   Mark slid into third and was safe.

5. **dive,** *v.*, to jump forward toward a base, to try to get a hand on it.*

   James was almost out, but he dove into home.

6. **tag out,** *phrasal verb*, to put out a runner by touching with a live ball.

   Ryan was tagged out when running to third.

7. **safe,** *adj.*, having reached a base before being put out.

   The first baseman dropped the ball, so Calvin was safe.

8. **out,** *adj.*, to fail when batting or running. Also a noun.*

   Strike three, you're out! That's two outs.

9. **steal,** *v.*, to advance a base without the help of a walk or batted ball.

If the pitcher throws a wild pitch, try to steal a base.

10. **pitchout,** *n.,* a defensive play where the pitch is thrown high and outside, so the batter cannot hit it. The catcher then jumps up, catches the ball, and throws it to second or third, to catch runners trying to steal a base.

If you think the runner is going to try to steal third, try a pitchout.

11. **pickoff,** *n.,* a defensive play where the pitcher throws a live ball to a fielder to stop a runner from stealing.

Mack threw a few pickoffs to keep the runners close to base.

12. **double play,** *n.*, a defensive play where two runners are put out.

Our team made two double plays in today's game.

13. **triple play,** *n.*, a defensive play where three runners are put out.

Garcia threw the ball to the catcher to complete the triple play.

14. **error,** *n.*, a mistake made by a fielder.

We lost the game because of too many errors in the field.

15. **rundown,** *n.*, a play where a runner is between two bases, and the two basemen throw the ball back and forth until they get close enough to tag the runner out.

Josh tried to steal a base but got caught in a rundown between first and second.

Diving to avoid being tagged out.

Language Notes:

1) **take a lead:** Sometimes the phrasal verb *lead off* is also used. *Lead off* also means to be the first batter in an inning.

2) **slide/dive:** Players slide or dive to make it difficult for fielders to tag them out. Youth baseball teaches players how to slide safely. As for the dive, many people argue whether it is a good play or not.

3) **outs:** Some ways players are put out:

- batters strike out (get three strikes).
- a batter hits a pop fly that is caught (called a *flyout*).
- fielders with a live ball touch bases before runners get there.
- fielders with a live ball tag runners out.

The Glove Is Mightier?

Left: Yankees' Babe Ruth slides into third, under Senators' third baseman Ossie Bluege, 1925.
Right: Washington fielder tags second ahead of a sliding runner and turns to throw to first,
to complete a double play.

There is a saying: More baseball games are won with the glove than with the bat. This means that the defense can win more often than the offense.

Knowing how to **field** is essential, and each player must know what to do in every **situation**. When a ball is hit, for example, players will move either toward the ball, toward a base, or toward a **backup** position.*

Teams also use different **strategies** to defend against some batters.* Most simply, if a slugger is at bat, the other team's manager may signal the outfielders to **shift** back, to be ready for a deep hit.

And there are bigger shifts that a defense can make. In 1948, the Cleveland Indians moved three infielders to the right of second base, to defend against a star left-handed batter, Ted Williams.

In recent years, the Tampa Bay Rays have **experimented** with new ways to shift. They studied where batters were likely to hit and shifted players to **cover** those areas. The strategy brought them to the **playoffs** more than once.*

When you understand how much there is to learn in baseball, you begin to see why players gain such a love for the game.

Baseball Facts

Honus Wagner is widely considered the No. 1 shortstop in baseball history, and he was one of the first five players to enter the Hall of Fame. Wagner played 21 seasons between 1897 and 1917, most of them with the Pittsburgh Pirates.

Dictionary

1. **field,** *v.*, to respond to a hit ball; to play the ball in the field.

   The coach says we need to improve our fielding.

2. **situation,** *n.*, the circumstances; the way something is.

   A first baseman must know what to do in every situation.

3. **backup,** *n.*, someone or something to help if needed.*

   The left fielder is the third baseman's backup. He'll back him up.

4. **strategy,** *n.*, a plan for winning a game or competition.*

   We're trying new fielding strategies.

5. **shift,** *v.*, to move. Also a noun.

   I'm not a good batter, so when I'm up, the outfielders shift forward.

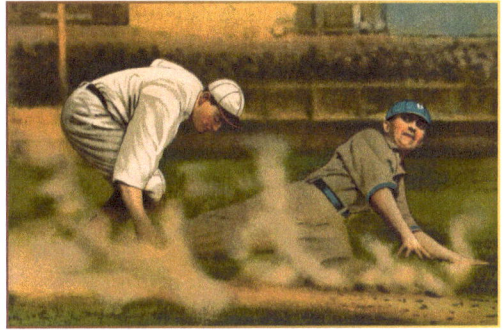

A 1911 baseball card, out at third base.

6. **experiment,** *v.*, to try new things to see how they work. Also a noun.

   Our manager wants to experiment with different strategies.

7. **cover,** *v.*, to protect an area or place, such as a base.

   If you play second base, be sure the cover the base well.

8. **playoff,** *n.*, a game or series in the postseason.*

   The Giants made it into the playoffs again this year!

Language Notes

1) **backup:** This noun is made from the phrasal verb *back up*. Such nouns are spelled either as one word or with a hyphen (back-up). A similar noun is *warmup*. Warmups are simple exercises people use to *warm up* (get physically ready).

2) **strategy:** Strategy comes from thinking. Games such as chess and backgammon are sometimes called strategy games.

3) **playoff:** Playoff games help decide which two teams will meet for a final championship. This noun also comes from a phrasal verb, *play off*, as in *The two teams will play off for third place*.

4) **The Glove Is Mightier?** The reading title refers to the proverb *The pen is mightier than the sword*, which means that words and talk achieve more than fighting.

Rain Check for First Run

Baseball Comics

We're playing the Yankees today, the best team. We're going to lose for sure.

We're **not** going to lose!

Reading about baseball won't help.

I'm not reading about baseball.

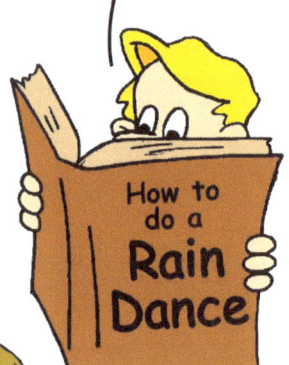

How to do a **Rain Dance**

Joey has just started playing baseball, and he is not the best player on his team. Here, he is telling his brother Sam how he nearly scored his first run.

Joey: I hit a single and almost scored my first run today.

Sam: Congratulations. Tell me about it.

Joey: Well, I hit a line drive into right field. And you should have seen me. I slid right into first.

Sam: You shouldn't slide into first base. It's faster to **run through** the base.*

Joey: I know. I forgot. But the first baseman was so surprised I slid, he dropped the ball.

Sam: Did you get to second?

Joey: Yeah, the pitcher threw a **wild pitch**, so I stole second.

Sam: Nice. What happened next?

Joey: The next batter was walked, so I **advanced** to third.

Sam: So the bases were loaded?

Joey: Yep. And I wanted to score, so I took a big lead off third.

Sam: That's not good.

Joey: It was OK. The pitcher tried a pickoff throw, but I dove back to touch the bag **just in time**.

Sam: If you got tagged out with the bases loaded, your coach would have been mad.

Joey: Yeah, but I didn't get tagged out.

Sam: Then what happened?

Joey: Well, Sam, our best batter, was up next, and I watched the pitcher throw a slow, easy pitch.

Sam: So you were sure to score!

Joey: Yeah, but just as Sam began to swing, we heard a loud clap in the sky.

Sam: Thunder?

Joey: Right. Suddenly it was raining hard. The game was **rained out**. So I didn't score.

Dictionary

1. **run through,** *phrasal verb*, to run straight over and beyond a base.*

   Remember, you can run through first base. You don't have to stop.

2. **wild pitch,** *n.*, a pitch that is out of control, so even the catcher cannot get it.

   If the pitcher throws a wild pitch, try to steal a base.

3. **advance,** *v.*, to move forward or upward.

   If you're on first base and the next batter is walked, you advance to second base.

When your game gets rained out.

4. **just in time,** *adv. phr.*, at the last minute; almost too late.

   We scored in the bottom of the ninth inning—just in time.

5. **rained out,** *adj. phr.*, to be canceled because of rain.

   If the weather gets much worse, the game will be rained out.

Language Notes

1) **run through:** Players are allowed to *run through* first base, meaning they can touch the base and run past it. At second and third, they must stop on the base.

2) **rain check:** This common idiom is used to decline invitations politely, as in *I'd like to come to dinner, but I'll have to take a rain check.* It comes from baseball, when games are rained out and tickets to future games are given to fans.

7. The Game and Score

Play Ball

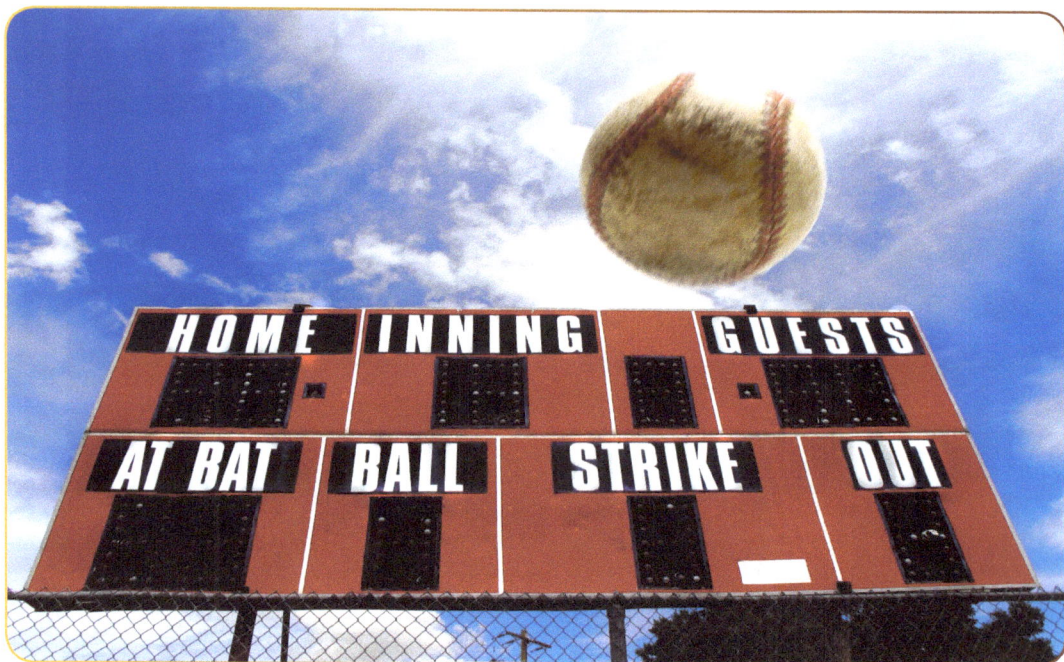

1. **score**, *n.*, the number of points two teams have. Also a verb, *to score*.

   What's the score? The score is four to two.

2. **scoreboard**, *n.*, a sign showing the score at a game.

   The scoreboard says the score is four to two.

3. **home team**, *n. phr.*, the team playing at its own ballpark. Also: *Home*.

   We're at home today, so we bat last.*

4. **visiting team**, *n. phr.*, a team playing at another's ballpark. Also: *Guests*.*

   Your team is the visiting team, so you bat first.

5. **inning**, *n.*, one of nine parts of a baseball game; counted with ordinals: first, second, third …*

   This is the ninth inning, so we have to score quickly.

6. **extra inning(s)**, *n. phr.*, innings added to a game if the score is tied at the end of the ninth inning.

   We were tied, so the game went into extra innings.

7. **top of**, *phr.*, the first half of an inning, when the visiting team bats.

   It is the top of the ninth (inning).*

8. **bottom of**, *phr.*, the second half of an inning; the home team bats.*

   It was the bottom of the sixth.

9. **error**, *n.*, a mistake made by a fielder.

Their team made a lot of errors, according to the scoreboard.

10. **win**, *n.*, a game that a team won. Compare with *loss*.

That team has the most wins in the league.

11. **loss**, *n.*, a game that a team lost. Compare with *win*.

Our team has eight wins and only two losses.

12. **tie**, *n.*, a game where both teams have the same score at the end. Also a verb and an adjective.

It was a three-to-three tie. We tied. It was a tie game.

13. **series**, *n.*, a group (often five or seven) of games played by two teams.

We're ahead in the series, three to one.

14. **tiebreaker**, *n.*, a game played to decide the winner of tied teams.

We're going to play a tiebreaker next week.

15. **on the road**, *adj. phr.*, playing at another team's field, in another place. Related: *road game*.

We're on the road next week, with a road game in San Francisco.

16. **shutout**, *n.*, a game in which one team does not score. In baseball, such a game with only one pitcher.*

We had two shutouts last year.

17. **no-hitter**, *n.*, a game in which one team scores no hits.

Our pitcher threw a no-hitter.

18. **perfect game**, *n.*, a game in which a team allows no hits, walks, or runs, and it has no errors and no hit batters.

We almost had a perfect game, but the other team scored in the ninth.

Language Notes:

1) **bat first/last:** In baseball, usually the visiting team bats first and the home team bats last.

2) **inning:** In each inning, each team gets to bat (until it has three outs).

3) **number of innings:** In youth baseball, games have six innings. But if one team is ahead by ten runs after four innings, the game ends early.

4) **top/bottom of:** Often the word *inning* is omitted, as in *We scored in the bottom of the ninth.*

5) **shutout:** This noun comes from the phrasal verb *shut out*, as in *The Cardinals shut us out yesterday; we were shut out.*

Baseball Becomes a Hit

Above: Metropolitan Baseball Nine, 1882. Facing (top): 1848-50 New York Knickerbockers, 1862 Reunion, 1862; Facing (bottom): Brooklyn Excelsiors, 1860.

Baseball most likely grew from a British game called **rounders**, a similar bat-and-ball game in which players run bases. The new American sport became a hit early on.

The earliest-known writing about baseball was a 1791 law that **banned** it near a building in Pittsfield, Massachusetts. The city wanted to **protect** its "newly built meeting house, particularly the windows," from sports that used balls. One of those sports was baseball.

In 1845, a team called the New York Knickerbockers was **founded**. This was an amateur club, but it established rules that helped create the game we play today.

The Knickerbocker Rules decided on nine-inning games, nine players per team, and bases that were 90 feet apart. New rules also banned "plugging" runners—a way to get runners out by **throwing** the ball *at* them.* Nowadays, of course, fielders have to tag or force runners out.

In 1857, 16 New York-area teams formed the National Association of Base Ball Players. By 1867, the **association** had 400 clubs, some as far away as California.

The first game for which **admission** was **charged** was played in 1858 in New York. Fans paid 50 cents' admission to see a matchup between two local teams.

Dictionary

1. **rounders,** *n.*, a British bat-and-ball game that came before baseball.

   Rounders, like baseball, uses a bat and ball and players run bases.

2. **ban,** *v.*, to make a rule against something; to say people can't do it. Also a noun.

   Players are banned from eating in the dugouts.

3. **protect,** *v.*, to keep something from being harmed or broken.

   Catchers wear gear to protect them from the ball.

4. **found,** *v.*, to start an organization, company, team, etc. A person who founds something is its *founder*.

   The first professional baseball team was founded in 1869 in Cincinnati.

5. **throw at,** *phrasal verb*, to throw something to try to hit someone or something with it.*

   James threw a water balloon at me.

6. **association,** *n.*, an organization or league of people, teams, etc.

   The Golden State Warriors are part of the National Basketball Association (NBA).

7. **charge admission,** *v. phr.*, to make people pay to get into an event.

   The school is charging admission to the baseball game.*

Language Notes

1) **throw at:** The difference between throw *at* and *to* is very important. If you throw a ball *to* players, you want them to catch it. If you throw it *at* them, you want it to hit them.

2) **admission:** The verb is *to admit*, meaning "to let someone enter," as in *Students will be admitted free.*

Baseball Facts

Daniel "Doc" Adams, a founder of the New York Knickerbockers, was a leader in making rules used today. He also helped create the short-stop position. A graduate of Harvard Medical School, he was a doctor when he played baseball, which was not yet a professional sport.

How to Name a Team

Baseball Comics

They hit every pitch over the fence. We can't stop them!

Don't worry. I'm training these birds to help.

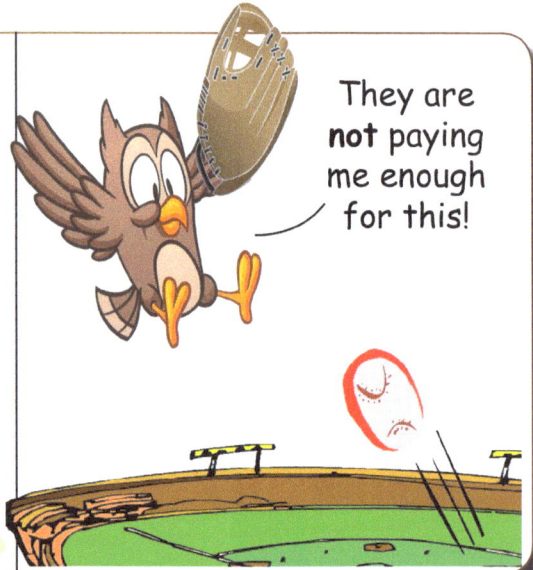

OUTFIELD
NO SLEEPING

They are **not** paying me enough for this!

Red is a baseball player, and he likes to tell **tall tales** *to his son Danny about games. Sometimes Danny doesn't believe his dad.*

Red: Did I ever tell you why our team is called the Cardinals?* We used to be called the Ducks.

Dan: Why did you change the name?

Red: Well, it was game seven, the final game in the 2002 **championship** series.*

Dan: So you were tied in the series?

Red: That's right. The championship was **on the line**.

Dan: What happened?

Red: Well, it was the bottom of the ninth, and we were up one run.

Dan: Yeah?

Red: And there were two outs, but our pitcher was real tired.

Dan: Oh no!

Red: Then one batter hit a single, and the next one got walked.

Dan: So there was a man on first and a man on second?

Red: Right. And our pitcher beaned the next batter.

Dan: So he got to go to first, and the bases were loaded! How exciting! What happened?

Red: Well, their next batter was a real slugger.

Dan: Wow! Two outs and the bases were loaded.

Red: Yeah, and that batter got a great hit. The ball was flying right over the fence—a home run **for sure**.

Dan: So the other team won?

Red: No! Just before the ball went over the fence, a bird flew by.

Dan: It hit a bird?!

Red: Yep, and then it fell down into an outfielder's glove. It was out. We won!

Dan: I don't believe it!

Red: And that bird was a pretty red cardinal. So we renamed the team after the poor bird.

Dan: Hey, I don't believe that!

Dictionary

1. **tall tale,** *n. phr.*, a story that is exaggerated or false.

   Our teacher likes to tell tall tales about when she was in school.

2. **championship,** *n.*, a game that will decide on a champion (winner).

   The championship game will be held next week.

3. **on the line,** *adj. phr.*, at risk, in danger.

   We have to score this inning; the game is on the line.

4. **for sure,** *adv. phr.*, certainly.

   Alan lost his glasses, so he's going to strike out for sure.

Baseball Facts

According to MLB rules, if a thrown or batted ball hits an animal such as a squirrel or a bird, it is still a live ball, just as if it had not touched the animal. And the game then continues.

Language Notes

1) **Cardinals:** The cardinal is a popular bird among teams: MLB's St. Louis Cardinals, the NFL's Arizona Cardinals, and numerous college and high school teams.

2) **Teams:** In American English, plural verbs are used with teams' mascots (The Cardinals *are* playing), but a singular verb is used with just the city name (St. Louis *is* playing).

8. Baseball Leagues

A Hit for All Ages

Tee Ball   Youth Baseball   College   Professional

Types and Levels of Leagues

1. **Youth Baseball:** There are numerous baseball leagues for children in North America and around the world. The largest and best-known is Little League Baseball, which has grown into an international league with teams in more than 80 countries.

2. **High School Baseball:** Baseball and softball are popular at high schools in North America, and many schools have excellent fields.

3. **College Baseball:** Men's baseball and women's softball are popular sports at U.S. colleges and universities, and both get TV time.

4. **Professional Baseball:** Baseball is the oldest major professional sport in North America, and pro leagues have been founded globally, in Latin America, Asia, Europe, and Australia. Professional baseball in North America consists of both Major League Baseball and Minor League Baseball (see No. 7).

5. **Amateur and Semi-Pro:** One of the reasons that baseball is so popular is people young and old can play, and little equipment is needed. As a result, there are leagues for amateurs and semi-professional players in North America and other countries.

Major League Baseball
Leagues:
- National League
- American League

Minor League Baseball
Classes:
- Triple-A (AAA)
- Double-A (AA)
- Class A (A)

College Baseball
Divisions:
- Division I
- Division II
- Division III

Little League Baseball
Divisions:
- Tee-Ball
- Minor League
- Little League (Major)
- Intermediate
- Junior/Senior

6. **Major League Baseball (MLB):** The American League (AL) was founded in 1901 and the National League (NL) was started in 1876. The two leagues joined to become a single organization in 2000. That organization also oversees Minor League teams.

7. **Minor League Baseball (MiLB):** Minor League Baseball teams are divided into five classes: Triple-A, Double-A, Class A, Class A Short Season, and Rookie. Many Minor League teams are affiliated with Major League clubs and train future Major League players for them.

8. **College Baseball:** In the U.S., college baseball is organized into three divisions for schools that have different levels of programs. Division I teams compete each year to win the College World Series in Omaha, Nebraska. Division II and Division III hold their own world series tournaments.

9. **Little League Baseball:** Little League Baseball is divided into divisions for kids of different ages. The best players in the Little League (Major) division compete in the Little League World Series each year in Williamsport, Pennsylvania, which draws kids from around the world. The older divisions, Intermediate through Big League, also compete in their own world series championships.

10. **Independent Leagues:** Many professional leagues have been started over the years that were not MLB or MiLB. Such leagues do not have to follow MLB rules, and they were once known as "outlaw leagues." Still, some of baseball's best players have played in these leagues.

Champions of All Ages

Players of the first World Series, 1903. The Boston Americans are in the front row; the Pittsburgh Pirates are in the back.

First World Series:
Americans vs. Pirates!

The first World Series was played in 1903 between the Boston Americans (now the Red Sox) and the Pittsburgh Pirates, with Boston winning—in an eight-game series. Since then, series of seven games have been played in all but three World Series (1919, 1920 and 1921).

The team with the most World Series wins is the New York Yankees, an American League team. The Yankees have 27 wins and also the most **appearances**, at 40.* In second **place** for the most wins are the Saint Louis Cardinals, who have won the World Series 11 times.*

The 2014 World Series champions, the San Francisco Giants, are No. 2 for the most appearances at 20. They are also No. 4 for the most wins, with 8.

In 2010, the Giants won the Series for the first time in 56 years. It was also the team's first World Series win since moving to San Francisco from New York in 1957.

Following the 2010 win, the Giants continued to **dominate**, winning three World Series **titles** in five years.

The Little League World Series

The first Little League World Series was played in 1947 in Williamsport, Pennsylvania, eight years after the first Little League game. A team from Williamsport won that first championship, playing against another Pennsylvania team. But soon, teams from far away were competing for the title in Williamsport each year.

Little League became international in 1951 when local leagues were started in Canada. Six years later, a pitcher named Angel Macias threw a perfect game, making Monterey, Mexico, the first non-U.S. team to win the championship. Teams from the Far East entered Little League in 1967, and the Little League World Series has been an international event since.

After the United States, Taiwan has the most wins. Taiwan won the Little League World Series 17 times in 27 years between 1969 and 1996. During the 1970s, teams from Taiwan won almost every year, and people there stayed up late at night to watch the games live on TV. Japan is No. 3 for the most wins, with 9.

As for U.S. teams, California leads for the most championships with seven wins, followed by Pennsylvania, Connecticut, and New Jersey, each with four.

Baseball Facts

Between 1884 and 1890, the National League and the American Association played championship series. Those series were promoted as the Championship of the United States and the World Championship Series, or "World Series" for short. This was how the word *world* came into the game.

Dictionary

1. **appearance,** *n.*, one time being seen or participating.*

   The new pitcher has made only two appearances on the mound so far.

2. **place,** *n.*, the order one is in in a competition.*

   The Yankees are in first place in the AL East division.

3. **dominate,** *v.*, (in sports) to win the most.

   For many years, Taiwan dominated the Little League World Series.

4. **title,** *n.*, a championship in a league or division.

   I'm sure we are going to win the division title this year.

Language Notes

1) **appearance:** The verb is *appear*, meaning "to be seen." The Yankees have appeared in the World Series 40 times, winning 27.

2) **place:** Ordinal numbers are used to show raking in competitions: *first place, second place, third place*, etc. . . . to last place.

The Hit to Remember

Baseball Comics

The principal said protective gear is essential for safety at a baseball game ...

Maybe I should wear a pitcher's helmet.

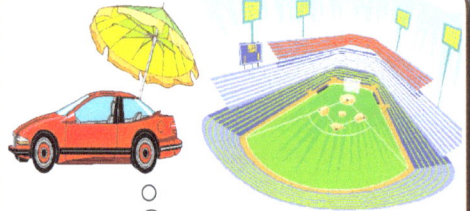

Protective gear is essential around baseball.

Ian and Joe played baseball together in high school, and today they are returning to their school to visit their old principal, Mr. Harris.

Ian: Mr. Harris will remember me better than he'll remember you.

Joe: That's not true.

Ian: He will. Mr. Harris was my Little League baseball coach.

Joe: Oh yeah?

Ian: Yeah. And when I played in high school, he attended all our games to **root for** me.*

Joe: Really?

Ian: Yeah. And I went to the local university, and I played college ball there.*

Joe: Did Mr. Harris watch your college games?

Ian: Yeah, he did. And our team won our division two years **in a row**.

Joe: Wow, so Mr. Harris was definitely a fan of yours.

Ian: After college, of course, I went pro. I joined the **big leagues**.

Joe: But you played for a team in another state.

Ian: He watched our games on TV. And after three years, I got **traded**. Then I was playing only an hour away.

Joe: Yeah, but I still think he's going to remember me more.

Ian: Ah, but I remember my big high school game.

Joe: The one where we won the championship?

Ian: Yep, and Mr. Harris was there when I hit the grand slam that won the game. He'll remember that for sure.

Joe: Yeah, but Mr. Harris was in the bleachers watching when I got *my* big hit, too.

Ian: *Your* big hit? When did you get a big hit?

Joe: It was that night I hit a foul ball over the fence and broke the **windshield** of Mr. Harris' BMW.

Ian: Oh, yeah. You're right. He *is* going to remember you better.

Dictionary

1. **root for,** *phrasal verb*, (1) to hope a person or team will win; (2) to show support by cheering.*

   We're rooting for the Giants in the World Series.

It's good to have someone rooting for you.

2. **in a row,** *adv. phr.*, consecutively, as in the same result each time.

   Fred has been late to baseball practice four times in a row.

3. **big league,** *n.*, the professional leagues of a sport. Also an idiom (see unit 9).

   Carl always dreamed of playing in the big leagues.

4. **trade,** *v.*, to send a player to another team in exchange for money or other players. Also a noun.

   My team traded me to the Cardinals. I got traded.

5. **windshield,** *n.*, the front window of a car.

   Karen's windshield got hit by a baseball.

Language Notes

1) **root for:** A similar word is *cheer (on)*, as in *The crowd cheered when I hit a home run*. Some American sports have *cheerleaders* to cheer the teams on.

2) **college ball / go pro:** *College ball* is an informal way to say college baseball, football, etc. *Go pro* is an informal way to say join a professional team.

9. Baseball Idioms

Sally really hit a home run with her new sales plan; she made a killing.

1. **ballpark figure,** *n. phr.*, an estimate; a number that is not correct, but is acceptable. Also: *ballpark estimate*.

   I can't give you a price on the work yet, but I can give you a ballpark figure.

   The mayor offered a ballpark estimate on how much a new airport would cost.

2. **bat around,** *phrasal verb*, to discuss, to debate. This baseball idiom goes back to the late 1800s. It uses the idea of batting balls around a field to mean "a back-and-forth discussion."

   The teachers batted around different plans for the school party.

   Our company has been batting around ideas for new products.

3. **bat a thousand,** *v. phr.*, to have a perfect record. If a baseball player is batting one thousand, he or she is hitting every pitch. This term is now used outside of baseball. Also: *batting one thousand*.

   Joe is batting a thousand on homework; he's gotten an A on every assignment.

   Tom is batting one thousand on getting to work on time.

4. **big league(s)**, *n.*, (1) somewhere where it is hard to compete; (2) the most famous of its kind. This idiom comes from baseball's major (big) leagues. Often used in the plural: *big leagues*.

Working for a big company is difficult; you're in the big leagues now.

The actress knew she was finally in the big leagues when she won an Oscar award.

5. **bush league**, *n.*, inferior; not professional. *Bush* here means "minor" (minor league). Also: *Bush leaguer* (n.), *bush-league* (adj.).

We looked bush league out on the baseball field today.

My boss made a bad decision; it was a bush-league decision.

6. **Charley horse**, *n.*, a sudden pain in the leg, often from exercise or sports. This idiom was first used in baseball.

Kim got a Charley horse and had to rest.

If you have a Charley horse, you need to stretch your leg.

7. **cover (one's) bases**, *v. phr.*, to do everything possible to prepare. Also: *cover all the bases*. From baseball, where players *cover* (guard) bases. Similar: *touch all bases*.

Kim eats well and exercises. She wants to cover all the bases.

The mayor covered all her bases during the election.

8. **down to (one's) last out**, *adj. phr.*, to have only one chance left. This idiom comes from baseball. If a team has two outs, it is *down to* only one last out. The phrase is used widely outside of baseball.

You've already gotten a bad grade on most of your tests; you're down to your last out in class.

Our company is almost out of money; we're down to our last out.

9. **drop the ball**, *v. phr.*, (1) to make a mistake; (2) to fail because you were not ready. This phrase comes from sports such as baseball, where a player drops a ball.

It is very important that you plan the birthday party well; don't drop the ball.

Kyle asked Sharon to marry him. She really dropped the ball when she said no; he would have been a great husband.

10. **early innings**, *n. phr.*, in the early stages. The phrase comes from the early part of a baseball game.

School started only two weeks ago. It's still early innings, so don't get too worried.

Scientists are researching the problem, but their research is still in the early innings.

11. **extra innings,** *n. phr.*, later than normal or expected. In baseball, when teams are tied at the end of the ninth inning, the game goes into additional, or extra, innings. This phrase is now used outside of baseball. *Extra-inning* can be used as an adjective.

Tom's extra-inning home run meant an extra-inning win for our team.

Talks between the two companies went into extra innings (lasted longer than expected).

12. **first base,** *n.*, the first step. From baseball, with first base being the first step to success. Often used with *get to.*

If the company offered you a job interview, you got to first base.

The company never looked at my résumé, so I never got to first base.

13. **glass arm,** *n. phr.*, an arm that becomes sore easily; an arm that cannot throw well.

Mark's a great batter, but he has a glass arm.

I can't pitch. I have a glass arm.

14. **go to bat for,** *v. phr.*, to defend or support someone. This slang term from the early 1900s comes from baseball, where one person bats when it is another person's turn.

The boss will be angry about your mistake, but I'll go to bat for you and say the mistake couldn't be avoided.

Stacy went to bat for her younger brother when he got into trouble in school.

15. **grand slam,** *n.*, a complete success. This idiom comes from a card game in the early 1800s and later was used in different sports. In baseball, it means a home run when the bases are loaded. It is now used outside of sports.

Our team won with a grand slam in the ninth inning.

The grand slam in golf is almost impossible to win.

16. **grandstand play,** *n. phr.*, an act of showing off, of trying to impress someone. This phrase comes from baseball, when a player tries to impress the people watching. *Grandstand* by itself can be a verb.

Jake always tries to make a grandstand play when our boss is in meetings.

The coach told Hal to stop grandstanding and be a team player.

17. **heavy hitter,** *n.*, a person or organization that is powerful. This phrase comes from sports such as baseball and boxing where certain players hit (slug) hard.

Sean is a heavy hitter in the banking industry.

Don't compete against her at work; she's a heavy hitter.

18. **home free,** *adj. phr.*, certain to succeed; knowing that you can succeed. This idiom probably comes from baseball, when a runner reaches home plate and knows he will not be out. It is now used widely for other subjects.

The teacher has only another ten tests to grade, so she is home free. She will finish on time.

Helen's job interview lasted for two hours, so they must want to hire her. I think she's home free.

19. **home run,** *n.*, a great achievement. Often used with the verbs *hit* and *score*. From baseball, when a batter hits the ball far enough to run around the bases and score a run.

Stacy hopes she'll hit a home run with her sales presentation.

Amy scored a home run when she bought a house in this neighborhood. It was a great investment.

20. **in the ballpark,** *adj. phr.*, an acceptable number, in an acceptable range. The opposite is *out of the ballpark*, meaning "an unacceptable number, one not in an acceptable range."

She wants thirteen thousand dollars for the car? That's in the ballpark. It isn't too expensive.

Two hundred dollars for a hotel room is out of the ballpark for me.

21. **in there pitching,** *adj. phr.*, trying hard; doing one's best to help. This idiom comes from baseball, where the pitcher is a key player.

When I was painting my house, Ian and Fred were in there pitching, helping me get it done.

Learning computers is hard, but stay in there pitching and you'll succeed.

22. **in scoring position,** *adj. phr.*, ready to succeed. This idiom comes from sports, where a team or a player is close to scoring.

Our company is in scoring position with our new products.

After a successful job interview, Jenny knew she was in scoring position for the job.

23. **in the same league,** *adj. phr.*, having the same skill level. This phrase comes from baseball, where players are in major or minor leagues depending on skill.

Vicky was afraid she wouldn't be in the same league as the other students in the school.

This restaurant isn't in the same league as the one we ate at last weekend.

24. knock out of the park, *v. phr.*, to be very successful. This idiom alludes to a batter hitting a ball out of a ballpark. Also *hit out of the park*.

Our company's new products are going to knock it out of the park.

Jenny really knocked it out of the park at her job interview.

25. major league, *n.*, the highest of its kind. In baseball, the highest leagues are the *major leagues*.

My boss was nervous because several major-league reporters were questioning him.

This is a major-league project. Are you sure you can do it?

26. minor league, *n.*, unimportant, not the highest. A related noun phrase is *minor leaguer*.

Don't worry so much over minor league problems. We have bigger problems to think about.

Go to the company president; don't just talk to some minor leaguer in the company.

27. ninth inning, *n. phr.*, the period near the end. From baseball, which has nine innings in a game. Also an adjective: *ninth-inning*.

Talks between the two countries are in the ninth inning.

Our company was going to hire Jenny, but she made a ninth-inning request for a higher salary.

28. off base, *adj. phr.*, (1) inaccurate; (2) inappropriate. From baseball, when a runner is not on the base.

Mark's explanation of this software is off base; it is incorrect.

Phil asked teacher to cancel the test because it was a sunny day; the teacher of course thought the suggestion was off base.

29. off base, *adv. phr.*, by surprise, unaware. Often used with *catch*.

The teacher's announcement that we were taking a test caught me off base. I hadn't studied.

Police officers always have to be on the ball. They can't let anything catch them off base.

30. on deck, *adj. phr.*, (1) in baseball, being the next in line to bat; (2) being available or ready. This idiom comes from people on the deck of a ship.

Several students were on deck to help clean up after the concert.

The boss wants everyone in the company to be on deck next week, if you need help.

31. on the ball, *adj. phr.*, (1) capable; (2) attentive; paying attention. *Have a lot on the ball* comes from baseball, where it once meant "to pitch with some spin, or with great speed." *On the ball* may come from sports such as baseball where players need to watch the ball closely.

You have to have a lot on the ball to work at this company (capable).

The police officers were on the ball and caught the robber quickly (attentive).

32. **out in left field,** *adj. phr.,* (1) completely wrong; (2) very strange or different. This idiom may have started because in some ballparks, the left field wall is farther away, or the left field is bigger.

All of Danny's answers on the test were out in left field. They were wrong.

The composer's music is unique; in fact, it's often out in left field.

33. **out of left field,** *adv. phr.,* unexpectedly or strangely. Often used with *come*.

The homework assign came out of left field, and Danny couldn't go to the game as planned.

My boss' complaints came out of left field; I thought he was happy with my work.

34. **out of (one's) league,** *adj. phr.,* (1) too difficult; (2) not right for a person. From sports like baseball, where players play in leagues that are appropriate for their skills.

When he started his new job, Tim quickly saw that he was out of his league. He wasn't good enough.

I think a car like this is out of your league; you're not rich.

35. **pinch hitter,** *n.,* a substitute, a replacement to help if needed. From baseball, where a pinch hitter bats for another player.

The school asked Amy to be a pinch hitter if any of the other teachers got sick.

I want our best salesman to work on this case, and have a pinch hitter ready in case something goes wrong.

36. **play ball,** *v. phr.,* (1) cooperate; (2) get started. In baseball, an umpire starts or restarts a game by shouting, "Play ball."

It's going to get dark in an hour. Let's play ball (get started).

We hoped the other company would work with us, but they wouldn't play ball (cooperate).

37. **play hardball,** *v. phr.,* to fight hard; to be willing to do bad things to gain something or win. From baseball, where a hardball is used.

Don't get into an argument at work with Jack; he plays hardball.

Tim was willing to play hardball to get the job.

38. **right off the bat,** *adv. phr.,* immediately. From baseball, with a ball being hit immediately.

The kids began eating the snacks at the party right off the bat.

I hit the ball right off the bat.

39. **rain check,** *n.*, a promise to accept an invitation but at a later time. Saying "I'll take a rain check" is a polite way to decline an invitation. This idiom comes from baseball, where games are stopped if it rains. People who paid to get in are given a *rain check* that lets them get into a future game.

You want to have lunch tomorrow? I'll have to take a rain check. I'm going to be in a meeting.

Ben asked me to dinner, but I said I'd have to take a rain check.

40. **second-guess,** *v.*, to criticize and offer advice. This verb comes from the noun *second guesser*. In baseball in the past, people unhappy with umpires called them "guessers." So a *second-guesser* was a fan who criticized umpires, players, or managers after a game. *Second-guess* is sometimes spelled with no hyphen.

My manager always wants to second-guess everything I do.

We need to stop second-guessing ourselves and get the job done.

41. **step up to the plate,** *v. phr.*, to offer to help; to be willing to do something. This idiom comes from baseball, with players walking (stepping) to the plate (home plate), where they try to hit the ball.

We need help raising money for our school trip; I hope a lot of students step up to the plate.

One of the reasons Paul got a raise is that he always steps up to the plate to help others.

42. **strike out,** *phrasal verb*, to fail. This idiom started in baseball, where a batter is out after getting three strikes. Today it is used outside of sports.

Shelly tried to get the teacher to let her retake the test, but she struck out.

Mark applied for a job at our company, but he struck out. We hired someone else.

43. **that's the way the ball bounces,** *clause*, an expression meaning "that is what happened and you must accept it." Also: *That's the way the cookie crumbles.*

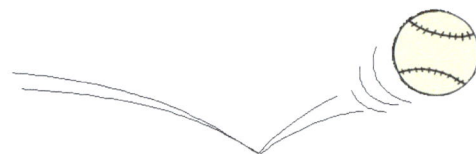

It's raining too hard to play baseball, but that's how the ball bounces.

Pat lost another baseball game, but that's how the cookie crumbles.

44. **this stage of the game (at),** *adv. phr.*, at this time; in this step of a process. Here, the *game* is the process or job being done. From sports. Also: *at this point (in time)*.

At this stage of the game, we don't know how much money our company will make.

With the history report due soon, Bill knew that at that stage of the game, it was too late to do more research.

45. **three strikes,** *n. phr.*, more mistakes than should be allowed. The *three strikes* idea from baseball is used widely outside baseball.

The mayor has made too many mistakes; it should be three strikes and you're out.

Our teacher has a three-strikes rule.

46. **throw a curve/curveball,** *v. phr.*, to surprise someone; to do something unexpected and win. This phrase comes from baseball, where a pitcher sometimes throws a *curve ball*, where the ball curves, making it difficult to hit.

The professor likes to throw students a curve by giving surprise quizzes.

My boss threw me a curve yesterday; she wants me to move to New York.

47. **touch bases (with),** *v. phr.*, to contact someone, to communicate. From baseball, when a batter touches the bases while running.

We'll touch bases outside after the meeting.

Be sure to touch bases regularly with colleagues who are also working on this project.

48. **two strikes against,** *phr.*, to be close to losing or having something bad happen; to already have two mistakes. This idiom comes from baseball, when a batter already has two strikes; if he gets a third, he will be out.

Carol had better not get into more trouble at work; she already has two strikes against her.

Vicky wanted to become manager, but she had two strikes against her, with all the mistakes she's made.

49. **whole new ballgame,** *phr.*, a situation that has changed completely. From baseball, when the lead has changed.

With a new teacher teaching her history class, Betty knew it was a whole new ballgame.

Now that I have money, I can fix up my house. It's a whole new ballgame.

50. **wild pitch,** *n.*, an action or statement that is careless. This expression comes from baseball, where a wild pitch is one that is out of control and cannot be caught.

Calling our baseball team the best anywhere—that's a wild pitch.

Our professor often throws out a wild pitch in his classes.

10. Quick Baseball Dictionary

achieve, *v.*, to accomplish something; to do something successfully. The noun is *achievement*. *Donny achieved a lot in baseball this year—he learned to hit better and field better.* **Achievement:** This can be both a count noun (many achievements) and a noncount noun (His achievement makes me proud).

advance, *v.*, to move forward or upward. *If you're on first base and the next batter is walked, you advance to second base.*

against (rules), *prep.*, not allowed, according to the rules or the law. *There's a rule against spitballs. They're against the rules.*

amazing, *adj.*, fantastic, hard to believe. *Mike is an amazing pitcher.* The verb is *to amaze*. The pitcher amazes me. He is *amazing*. I was *amazed* when I watched.

assistant coach, *n. phr.*, a coach who helps a manager. *Our manager is sick, so the assistant coach is the boss today.*

association, *n.*, an organization or league of people, teams, etc. *The Golden State Warriors are part of the National Basketball Association (NBA).*

at-bat, *n.*, a turn trying to hit. The plural is *at-bats*. *Barry had three at-bats today, and he got a hit at each.* As a noun, the term is spelled either with a hyphen or as two words: at-bat, at bat(s).

backup, *n.*, someone or something to help if needed. *The right fielder will be the first baseman's backup. He'll back him up.* This noun is made from the phrasal verb *back up*. Such nouns are spelled either as one word or with a hyphen (back-up). A similar noun is *warmup*. Warmups are simple exercises people use to *warm up* (get physically ready) for a sport, etc.

bag, *n.*, the square white markers on first, second and third bases. *Keep your foot on the bag or you'll get tagged out.*

ball, *n.*, a bad pitch, which a batter cannot likely hit. *OK, we have two balls and one strike.*

ban, *v.*, to make a rule against something; to say people can't do it. Also a noun. *Players are banned from eating in the dugouts.*

base, *n.*, a spot runners must pass to score a run, as in *first base, second base,* and *third base.* Often just the number is used, as in *There's a runner on first.*

baseball, *n.*, the ball used in baseball. *All youth baseball games must use regulation baseballs.*

baseball hat, *n. phr.*, a cap used in baseball, with a visor that keeps the sun out of a person's eyes. Also called a baseball cap. *Wear a baseball hat to keep the sun out of your eyes.*

baseball pants, *n. phr.*, pants worn by baseball players. *Our baseball pants have a stripe on the leg.*

baseball uniform, *n. phr.*, clothes with the same colors/patterns worn by a group of people such as a sports team. *For uniforms this year, we have red shirts and striped pants.*

bat, *n.*, the stick used to hit baseballs. *Never throw the bat after you hit the ball. Drop it before you run.*

batter, *n.*, a player who bats. *Hank is the first batter, and Gina is the second batter.*

batter's box, *n. phr.*, a box where batters stand to bat. There is a box for left-handed batters and one for right-handed batters. *Step out of the batter's box and rest between pitches.*

batting gloves, *n. phr.*, gloves worn by batters. *Put on your batting gloves.*

batting helmet, *n. phr.*, a plastic helmet worn to protect a batter's head. *Batting helmets are essential for batters' safety.*

bean, *v.*, to hit on the head, especially with a baseball. *Hank got beaned by a batted ball the last time he played pitcher.*

beat, *v.*, to win. *When our pitcher is hot, we beat other teams easily.* This is one of many informal terms meaning "to win" or "to win over someone." Many of these terms are colorful: *kill, squash, destroy, stomp, wipe out,* etc.

beginner, *n.*, someone who has just started doing something. *Jake is a beginner at baseball.*

big leagues, *n.*, the professional leagues of a sport. Also an idiom (See unit 9). *Carl always dreamed of playing in the big leagues.*

bleachers, *n.*, simple outdoor benches for people to sit and watch games. These are common at school fields. *We sat in the bleachers.*

blocking, *n.*, (catchers) using their body to stop pitches that hit the ground, or are "in the dirt." *If the ball is in the dirt, don't try to catch it; block the pitch instead.*

bottom, *n.,* the second half of an inning, when the home team bats. *It was the bottom of the sixth.* Often the word *inning* is omitted, as in *We scored in the bottom of the ninth.*

breaking ball, *n. phr.,* a pitch in which the ball moves to the side or down. *Jim's breaking ball often fools batters.*

bullpen, *n.,* (1) a place at a field where pitchers warm up. Also called *the pen*; (2) the relief pitchers on a baseball team. *Our bullpen failed us in yesterday's game; no one pitched well.* Pitchers can warm up (get ready to play) by throwing practice pitches in the bullpen, an area where they will not be hit by the ball during a game.

bunt, *v.,* to hold a bat out and let a pitch hit it, usually as a surprise. *If you bunt, you'll help advance a runner.* When players bunt, it is often a *sacrifice bunt*—they may not reach first base, but will help other players advance.

calculate, *v.,* to count; to find a number. The noun is *calculation. Ben calculates he will throw more than five hundred pitches during the year.*

call the game, *v. phr.,* to choose what pitches are thrown. *Our coach will call the game.*

career, *n.,* a person's lifetime work, as in *She retired after a twenty-year career in business.* For professional athletes, the term refers to their time playing a sport, as in *Babe Ruth's 22-year career.*

catcher, *n.,* a player who catches pitches. *Catchers work harder than anyone. Catchers use catcher's mitts and special gear.*

catcher's box, *n. phr.,* an area behind home plate where a catcher crouches to play. *The catcher crouches behind home plate, in the catcher's box. The umpire crouches behind him.*

catcher's gear, *n. phr.,* equipment worn by catchers for protection. *Catcher's equipment protects you when you get hit by the ball.*

catcher's helmet, *n. phr.,* a special helmet and facemask worn by a catcher for protection. *Many catchers throw their helmets off when they need to see better.*

catcher's mitt, *n. phr.,* a padded glove used to protect a catcher's hand. *A catcher's mitt is thick to protect the catcher's hand.*

center field, *n.,* the area of a field beyond the bases and straight ahead of a batter. *Kyle is the center fielder. He's playing center field.*

center fielder, *n.,* a player who covers center field. *The center fielder caught the ball. Paul, you're the center fielder, not the left fielder.*

championship, *n.,* a game that will decide on a champion (winner). *The championship game will be held next week.*

chance, *n.,* a time to try something; an opportunity. *Everyone will get a chance to bat.* In youth sports, teams talk about giving all players a *chance* to play.

changeup, *n.,* a pitch that's slower, to fool a batter. Also: *slowball. Lester is practicing changeups.*

charge admission, *v. phr.,* to make people pay to get into an event. *The school is charging admission to the baseball game.* **Admission:** The verb is *to admit*, meaning "to let someone enter," as in *Students will be admitted free.*

chest protector, *n. phr.,* a pad that catchers wear on their chest for protection. *Make sure the chest protector is on tight.*

circumference, *n.,* the distance around a round object, or a circle. *The circumference of a baseball is 9 inches.*

cleats, *n.,* shoes with spikes on the bottom. Also, the spikes themselves. *Cleats help players run faster.*

closer, *n.,* a relief pitcher who specializes in getting the final outs in a game. This often is a team's best relief pitcher. *With a two-run lead, they're putting in their closer.*

coach, *n.,* a person who manages a baseball team. The head coach in baseball is called the *manager*. Other coaches include: *assistant coach, first-base coach, third-base coach, pitching coach, hitting coach, bench coach, trainers.*

coach's box, *n. phr.,* a box next to first or third base for base coaches. *Base coaches stand in the coaches' boxes to help batters.*

compare, *v.,* to look at two things to see how they are similar, different, or better. *Compare these two bats and see which one you like better.*

competitive, *adj.,* (1) hard to win; (2) wanting very much to win.* *Baseball is a very competitive sport—players try hard to win.* The verb is *compete*, as in *The teams compete to see which is the best.* The noun is *competition*, as in *We had a batting competition to see who could hit the most pitches.*

contact, *n.,* the touching of other people. Used here as an adjective. *American football and rugby are contact sports.* A contact sport is one where players have contact with each other, such as American football and rugby. In contact sports, players are more likely to get hurt.

count, *n.,* the number of balls and strikes a batter has. *What's the count? The count is three and two?* **Full count:** If a batter has three balls and two strikes, it is called a *full count.*

cover, *v.,* to protect an area or place, such as a base. *If you're going to play second base, be sure the cover the base well.*

crouch, *v.,* to bend your knees so you are closer to the ground. *The catcher crouches behind the batter to catch the pitch.*

curveball, *n.,* a pitch that curves as it flies to the plate, making it more difficult to hit. *Hank threw a curveball, not a fastball.* When two-word nouns become very common, they are often spelled as one word. Sometimes, they are spelled in different ways: *curveball / curve ball; knuckleball / knuckle ball.*

defense, *n.,* a team when it is on the field trying to stop the other team from scoring. *Our team plays great on defense, but poorly on offense.* Many sports have an *offense* (trying to score points) and *defense* (trying to stop scoring). Note the American English spellings. In British English, an S is used instead of the C: *defence, offence.*

defensive, *adj.,* on defense, trying to stop a team from scoring. *George is a good defensive player.*

design, *v.,* to plan something with a certain goal. *They designed the ballpark to make it hold lots of fans.*

diameter, *n.,* the distance through the middle of a round object or circle. *The diameter of a baseball bat is 2.75 inches.*

diamond, *n.,* a square with one corner pointing up. A baseball diamond is the main part of a baseball field. *These are the measurements for a baseball diamond.*

dive, *v.,* to jump forward toward a base while running, to try to get a hand on it. *James was almost out, but he dove into home.* Players slide or dive to make it more difficult for fielders to tag them out. Youth baseball teaches players how to slide safely. As for the dive, many people argue whether it is a good play or not.

double, *n.,* a hit that allows a batter to run to second base. *Sanchez is going to get a double with of that hit.*

double play, *n.,* a defensive play where two runners are put out. *Our team made two double plays in today's game.*

drive in, *phrasal verb,* to hit the ball and help another player score a run. *Try to drive in the runner on third.*

dugout, *n.,* a place where players sit when they are not playing.

error, *n.,* a mistake made by a fielder. This is an important statistic. *They scored a lot of errors, according to the scoreboard. We lost the game because of too many errors.*

exact, *adj.,* correct in every way. *All the distances on the baseball field must be exact.*

experience, *n.,* skill in a job or sport because you have done or played it before. *Jim has a lot of experience as a baseball manager.* Experience here is an uncountable noun, as in much *much experience* or *a little experience. I have experience at baseball. I have experience pitching.*

experiment, *v.,* to try new things to see how they work. Also a noun. *Our manager wants to experiment with different strategies.*

extra inning(s), *n. phr.,* innings added to a game if the score is tied at the end of the ninth inning. *We were tied, so the game went into extra innings.*

fair, *adj.,* (a hit ball) inside the foul line. Also: *fair ball. It's a fair ball! It was inside the foul line. Run to first!*

fastball, *n.,* a pitch that is thrown as fast as possible, to make it difficult to hit. *Randy has a great fastball. Jim's fastball is hard to hit.*

feat, *n.,* an achievement; something that is difficult to do. *Maintaining a batting average of three fifty (.350) is a rare feat.*

field, *v.,* to respond to a hit ball; to play the ball in the field. *The coach says we need to field better. We need to improve out fielding.*

first base, *n.,* the first spot a runner must reach. *I threw the ball to first base before the runner got there.*

first-base coach, *n. phr.,* a coach who stands near first base and helps runners. *The first base coach tells runners what to do as they pass first. Watch the first base coach when you're running to first.*

first baseman, *n.,* a player who covers first base. *John is our first baseman. Throw it to the first baseman.*

fool, *v.,* to make someone believe something. *He fooled me with a fastball.*

for sure, *adv. phr.,* certainly. *Alan lost his glasses, so he's going to strike out for sure.*

foul, *n., adj.,* a hit ball that goes outside the foul line. Also: *foul ball. Fred hit four foul balls before getting on base.*

foul line, *n.*, lines between home and first base and home and third. *The ball rolled outside the foul line.* Balls must be hit within the foul lines. Balls that are hit outside are called *foul balls*, or *fouls*, and they count as strikes.

found, *v.*, to start an organization, company, team, etc. A person who founds something is its *founder*. *The first professional baseball team was founded in 1869 in Cincinnati.*

framing, *n.*, (catchers) holding the catcher's mitt inside the strike zone, to make pitches look like strikes. *Sam's learning to frame pitches, so umpires will call more strikes.*

gear, *n.*, tools. For baseball, both *gear* and *equipment* are commonly used. *Remember to bring your baseball gear to the game.*

glass arm, *n. phr.*, an arm that gets tired easily and cannot throw a baseball well. *Kyle is a great batter, but he has a glass arm.*

glove / fielding glove, *n.*, a padded glove used by baseball players on defense. *Tim is left-handed, so he wears a glove on his right hand.*

grand slam, *n.*, a home run when all three bases have runners. *A grand slam now would give us four points and we'd win.*

gross, *adj.*, disgusting. *The dugout has not been cleaned all year; it is really gross.*

hand signal, *n. phr.*, a secret gesture with your hand to tell someone something. *The pitcher waited for the catcher's hand signal.*

hard, *adj.*, able to cause damage to; destructive to. *The way catchers crouch can be hard on their knees.*

hard, *adj.*, difficult; *adv.*, to do something with a lot of effort. *Playing baseball is hard, but we work hard at it.*

hit, *v.*, to strike a ball with a bat. Also a noun. *Jim hasn't been able to hit the ball all day. He has had no hits.*

hold, *v.*, to have and/or maintain a record. *For a long time, Babe Ruth held the record for the most home runs.*

home plate, *n.*, the plate where a batter bats. *Kate pitched the ball right over home plate.*

home run, *n.*, a hit that allows a batter to run all three bases and back to home plate. *Eric hit two home runs today. We call Eric the Home Run King.*

home team, *n. phr.*, the team playing in its own ballpark. Also: *Home. We're at home today, so we*

bat last. **Bat first/last:** In baseball, the visiting team bats first and the home team last.

in a row, *adv. phr.*, consecutively, as in the same result each time. *Fred has been late to baseball practice four times in a row.*

infield (infielder), *n.*, the part of the field within the bases. *The shortstop plays in the infield.*

inning, *n.*, one of nine parts of a baseball game; counted with ordinal numbers: first, second, third … *This is the ninth inning, so we have to score quickly.* In each inning, each team gets to bat (until it has three outs). **Number of innings:** In youth baseball, games have six innings. But if one team is ahead by ten runs after four innings, the game ends early.

intentional walk, *n. phr.*, a walk when a pitcher throws four balls on purpose. When powerful batters are up, teams sometimes walk them on purpose, especially if there is a runner on third, who could score with a hit.

in the dirt, *adv./adj. phr.*, a pitch that hits the ground is often said to be "in the dirt."

jersey, *n.*, a shirt worn by an athlete. *Our team has our names on our jerseys.*

just in time, *adv. phr.*, at the last minute; almost too late. *We scored in the bottom of the ninth inning—just in time.*

knuckleball, *n.*, a pitch with no spin, so its path is hard to predict. *I'll teach you how to throw a knuckleball.*

lead, *v.*, to control people, to tell them what to do. *Our manager leads our team well.*

leather, *n.*, animal skin used for shoes, etc. Also an adjective. *Most baseball gloves are made of leather.*

leave on base, *v. phr.*, to still be on base after three outs, and therefore unable to score. *Two men were left on base when I struck out.*

left-handed, *adj.*, used to using your left hand. The opposite is *right-handed*. *Are you right-handed or left-handed? I'm right-handed.* Also: *left-hander.*

left field, *n.*, the area of a field beyond the bases and to the batter's left. *Jake is in left field today. He's playing left field.*

left fielder, *n.*, a player who covers left field. *Donny is usually our left fielder. Who wants to be the left fielder?*

leg guards, *n.*, pads that catchers wear on their legs for protection. *Leg guards protect a catcher's knees and lower legs.*

let down, *phrasal verb*, to fail to support someone; to disappoint. *We know our coach will always help. He never lets us down.*

line drive, *n.*, a batted ball that goes straight, close to the ground. *Victor hit a line drive to left field and ran to first.*

loss, *n.*, a game that a team did not win. *Our team has three wins and only one loss.*

maintain, *v.*, to keep something; to keep something at a certain level. *Ned maintained a batting average of two fifty (.250).*

make a pitch, *v. phr.*, an idiom meaning "to speak to promote something." If you make a pitch, you try to convince people of something. *The car salesman made his pitch.*

manager, *n.*, the head coach on a baseball team. *Our manager has put together a great team.*

measurement, *n.*, a number showing size, from measuring something. *Here are the measurements for the baseball field.*

miss, *v.,* to swing but not hit a ball; to fail to hit something. *That pitcher's changeups are easy to miss.*

no-hitter, *n.*, a game in which one team scores no hits. *Our pitcher threw a no-hitter.*

on-deck circle, *n. phr.*, a circle where the next batter in line waits to bat. *Wait in the on-deck circle to bat.*

on deck, *adj. phr.,* next in line to bat. *Smith is batting, and Sanchez is on deck.*

on the line, *adj. phr.*, at risk, in danger. *We have to score this inning; the game is on the line.*

on the road, *adj. phr.*, playing at another team's field, in another place. *We're on the road next week; we're playing in San Francisco.* Related: *road game.*

out, *adj.*, to fail when batting or running. Also a noun. *Strike three, you're out! That's two outs.*

outfield, *n.*, the part of the field beyond the bases. *Vick always hit into the outfield.*

outfielder, *n.*, a player who plays outside the bases, in the outfield. *George is usually an outfielder.*

overhand, *adv./adj.*, to throw a ball above your shoulder. *Jill's overhand pitch is very good.*

pad, *v.*, to add soft material, for protection. Also a noun: *pad, padding. Early baseball gloves were padded with just pieces of leather.*

perfect game, *n. phr.*, a game in which the other team has no hits, walks, or runs, and your team has no errors and no hit batters. *We almost had a perfect game, but the other team scored in the ninth.*

pickoff, *n.*, a defensive play where the pitcher throws a live ball to a fielder to stop a runner from stealing. *Mack threw a few pickoffs to keep the runners close to base.*

pitch, *v.*, to throw a baseball over home plate so a batter can try to hit it. Also a noun. *Jim pitched for seven innings. He threw a lot of pitches.*

pitch (types). Other names for pitches include **fastballs:** cutter, four-seam, two-seam, sinker; **breaking balls:** curveball, knuckle curve, screwball, slider; **changeups:** circle changeup, forkball, palmball.

pitcher, *n.*, a player who pitches. *Tom is the pitcher on our team. Cy Young was a pitcher on five teams.* Note: *Pitcher, catcher,* and *batter* come from the verbs *pitch, catch,* and *bat.*

pitcher's mound, *n. phr.*, a small hill (mound) where a pitcher pitches from. *Hey, Sam, take the mound (= go out and pitch).*

pitchout, *n.*, a defensive play where the pitch is thrown high and outside, so the batter cannot hit it. The catcher jumps up, catches the ball, and throws it to second or third, to catch a runner trying to steal. *If you think the runner's going to try to steal third base, try a pitchout.*

playoff, *n.*, a game or series in the postseason. *The Giants made it into the playoffs again!* Playoff games usually help decide which two teams will meet for a final championship. This noun comes from a phrasal verb, *play off*, as in *The two teams will play off for third place.*

pop fly, *n.*, a ball hit high in the air. Also called a *fly ball. The coach told the kids practice catching pop flies.*

position, *n.*, a player's job, such as the pitcher or the catcher. *Catchers have the most difficult position.*

practice, *n.*, a time when sports teams try to improve. Also a verb. *We have baseball practice after school every day.*

prefer, *v.*, to like something better, to want it more than another. *Leslie prefers watching baseball to football.*

protect, *v.*, to keep something from being harmed or broken. *Catchers wear gear to protect them from the ball.*

put in, *phrasal verb*, to send a player into a game to play. The opposite is *take out. The coach* took Ed out of the game and put Paul in to re-place him after two innings.

rain check, *n.*, a common idiom used to decline invitations politely, as in *I'd like to come to dinner, but I'll have to take a rain check.* The phrase comes from baseball, when games are rained out and tickets (rain checks) to future games are given to fans.

rained out, *adj. phr.*, to be canceled because of rain. *If the weather gets much worse, the game will be rained out.*

RBI, *n.*, run batted in. The plural is *RBIs. Carl had four RBIs today.*

record, *n.*, a number showing the most of something. Common verbs used with it are *set, break,* and *hold*, as in *I set a new record. I broke the old record and now I hold the record.*

relief pitcher, *n. phr.*, a pitcher who comes in after a starting pitcher. *Ned was a starting pitcher last year, but this year, he's a relief pitcher.* **Relief:** Someone who takes another person's place at a job, as in *I can't go home until my relief arrives.*

right field, *n.*, the area of a field beyond the bases and to the batter's right. *Timmy caught two fly balls in right field.*

right fielder, *n.*, a player who covers right field. *Kate was our right fielder today. A right fielder must be able to catch the ball while running.*

root for, *phrasal verb*, (1) to hope a person or team will win; (2) to show support by cheering. *We're rooting for the Giants in the World Series.*

roster, *n.*, a list showing what players play what positions. *We're going to have a new player on our roster next month.* In MLB baseball, there is a main, 25-man roster and a 40-man roster.

rule, *n.*, an instruction saying what you can or cannot do. *You must always follow the rules; never break the rules.*

run, *n.*, a point scored in baseball. The plural is *runs. We scored seven runs already.*

rundown, *n.*, a play where a runner is between two bases, and the two basemen throw the ball back and forth until they get close enough to the runner to tag him out. *Josh tried to steal a base but got caught in a rundown between first and second.*

run through, *phrasal verb*, to run straight over and beyond a base. *Remember, you can run through first base. You don't have to stop.* Players are allowed to *run through* first base, meaning they can touch the base and run past it. At second and third, they must stop on the base.

safe, *adj.*, having reached a base before being put out. *The first baseman dropped the ball, so Calvin was safe.*

score, *n.*, the number of points two teams have. Also a verb, *to score. What's the score? The score is four to two.*

scoreboard, *n.*, a sign showing the score at a baseball field. *The scoreboard says the score is four to two.*

season, *n.*, the period of time in which a league plays each year. For MLB baseball, the season usually goes from April through September. The postseason then is in October.

second base, *n.*, the second base a runner must reach. *Jimmy plays second base; he's the second baseman.*

second baseman, *n.*, a player who covers second base. *I'm usually the second baseman. Jenny wants to be the second baseman.*

secret, *adj.*, something other people don't know. Also a noun. *Kenny has a secret pitch that can fool batters.*

series, *n.*, a group (often five or seven) of games played by two teams. *We're ahead in the series three to one.*

shift, *v.*, to move. Also a noun. *I'm not good at batting, so when I'm up, the outfielders shift forward.*

shortstop, *n.*, a player who covers the middle of the infield. *A shortstop must be agile and fast. Many balls are hit toward the shortstop, so he must be fast.*

shutout, *n.*, a game in which one team does not score. In baseball, such a game with only one pitcher. *We had two shutouts last year.* This noun comes from the phrasal verb *shut out*, as in *The Cardinals shut us out yesterday; we were shut out.*

signal, *n.*, to use a gesture to communicate. Also a verb. *The catcher signals the batter to tell him what pitch to throw.*

single, *n.*, a hit that allows the batter to run to first base. *Ralph hit two singles today.*

situation, *n.*, the circumstances; the way something is. *A first baseman must know what to do in every situation.*

slide, *v.*, to fall back onto the ground while running, to try and get a foot on a base. *Mark slid into third and was safe.* Players slide or dive to make it more difficult for fielders to tag them out. Youth baseball teaches players how to slide safely. As for the dive, many people argue whether it is a good play or not.

slider, *n.*, a pitch that flies to the side and down. *Frank has been having trouble hitting sliders.*

slugger, *n.*, a very good batter in baseball, who can hit very hard. *That team has some real sluggers.* The verb *to slug* means "to hit hard." A very good boxer is called a slugger, as it a good batter.

snackbar, *n.*, a place that sells foods and drinks. For many young players, this is their favorite part of a ballpark. *Let's hit (go to) the snackbar and get something to drink.*

softball, *n.*, a form of baseball that uses a larger and softer ball. *Rita is going to join her company's softball team.* Softball is a popular sport in schools and universities, as well as for adults who are not professional players. Many companies have softball teams.

spectacular, *adj.*, amazing; amazing to watch. *Bob had a spectacular season this year.*

spitball, *n.*, a pitch when the ball has been spit on to change how it flies. *Hank got into trouble for throwing a spitball. They're against the rules.*

standard, *n.*, a measurement everyone must follow. Also and adjective. *The baseball league sets standards for the size and weight of balls.*

state, *n.*, one of the fifty states in the U.S. *Our team won the state championship last year.*

steal, *v.*, to run to the next base without the batter hitting the ball. *If the pitcher throws a wild pitch, try to steal a base.*

step on, *phrasal verb*, to put your foot onto something. *Be careful; don't step on your bag.*

strategy, *n.*, a plan for winning a game or competition. *We're trying new fielding strategies.* Strategy comes from thinking. Games such as chess and backgammon are called strategy games.

strike, *n.*, a pitch inside the strike zone that is not hit. Also, a pitch outside that is swung at but not hit. *Our pitcher threw almost all strikes today.*

strike out, *phrasal verb,* to be out on three strikes. Noun: *strikeout. Ben rarely strikes out, but he struck out today.*

strike zone, *n.*, a space above home plate and between a batter's knees and chest. *The pitch was inside the strike zone, so it was a strike.*

swing, *v.*, to move the bat to try to hit the ball. Also a noun. *Swing a few times before entering the batter's box. Take a few swings.*

tag out, *phrasal verb*, to be put runners out by touching them with a live ball. *Ryan was tagged out when running to third.*

take a lead, *v. phr.*, to step off a base before a pitch is thrown, to move closer to the next base. Also: lead off the base. Sometimes the phrasal verb *lead off* is also used. *Young players need to learn how to take leads. Lead off the base! Lead off* also means to be the first batter for a team or in an inning. Also: the *leadoff batter.*

tall tale, *n. phr.*, a story that is exaggerated or false. *Our teacher likes to tell tall tales about when she was in school.*

teammate, *n.*, another person on the same team. *The coach took me and my teammates out to pizza after the game.* A *mate* is a friend. The word by itself is common in British and Australian English. In American English it is often used with other words: teammate, classmate, roommate, etc.

third base, *n.*, the third spot a runner must reach. *When the outfielder dropped the ball, Mike made it to third base.*

third-base coach, *n. phr.*, a coach who stands near third base and helps runners. *I'll be the third-base coach today. The third-base coach signaled Hal to run for home.*

third baseman, *n.*, a player who covers third base. *Ted is a good third baseman. Third basemen must have strong arms.*

throw at/to, *phrasal verb*, to throw something to try to hit someone or something. *James threw a water balloon at me.* The difference between *throw at* and *to* is very important. If you throw a ball *to* a player, you want him to catch it. If you throw it *at* him, you want it to hit him.

tie, *n.*, a game where both teams have the same number of points. *Tie* is also an adjective and a verb. *It was a three-to-three tie. It was a tie game. The two teams tied.*

tiebreaker, *n.*, a game that will decide the winner of tied teams. *We're going to play a tiebreaker next week.*

tire out, *phrasal verb*, to become weak or tired after work or exercise; to make weak or tired. *New players often tire out easily and quickly.*

top, *n.*, the first half of an inning, when the visiting team bats. *It is the top of the ninth (inning).* Often the word *inning* is omitted, as in *We scored in the top of the ninth.*

trade, *v.,* to send a player to another team in exchange for money or other players. Also a noun. *My team traded me to the Cardinals. I got traded.*

triple, *n.,* a hit that allows a batter to run to third base. *Jake hit a triple and nearly got to home plate.*

triple play, *n.,* a defensive play where three runners are put out. *Sanchez threw the ball to the catcher to complete the triple play.*

trip over, *phrasal verb,* to fall because your foot hits something. *Pete tripped over the bat. Trip is a transitive verb (Joe tripped me and I fell) and an intransitive verb (I tripped and fell). Add over to say what the foot hit, as in I tripped over the cat.*

umpire, *n.,* a person who judges plays in baseball. *An umpire must have a good eye to make good calls. The umpire is always right. Never argue with an umpire.* The main umpire is the *home plate umpire.* A game may also have a *field umpire.* People sometimes called umpires "blue" because of the color of the uniforms they usually wear.

underhand, *adv./adj.,* (a ball) thrown with your hand moving from low to high. *Show me how to pitch underhand.*

visiting team, *n. phr.,* a team playing at another's ballpark. Also: Guests. *Your team is the visiting team, so you bat first.* **Bat first/last:** In baseball, usually the visiting team bats first and the home team last.

walk, *n.,* a free walk to first base because the pitcher throws four balls. Also a verb. *We got a lot of walks in today's game.*

walk off, *phrasal verb,* to walk around to recover from an illness. *When Jenny got beaned, the coach told her to walk it off.* In youth sports, when players are hurt but not seriously, a coach or a parent will often them to "walk it off."

wild pitch, *n.,* a pitch that is out of control, and even the catcher can't get it. *If he throws a wild pitch, you should try to steal a base.*

win, *n.,* a game that a team won, or got the most points in. *That team has the most wins in the league.*

windshield, *n.,* the front window of a car. *Karen's windshield got hit by a baseball.*

yarn, *n.,* thread used for knitting, as in knitting a sweater. *Some early baseballs were made with yarn.*

Notes:

_____

_____

_____

_____

_____

_____

_____

_____

_____

_____

_____

_____

Books from Targets in English

English for Baseball

English Idioms: Money—Hit the Jackpot

English Idioms: Sports—Hit a Home Run

English Idioms: Foods—Going Bananas

English Idioms: Study—Hit the Books

English Idioms: Body—Thumbs Up

English Idioms: Colors—Seeing Red

English Idioms: Emotions—Laugh Your Head Off

English Idioms: Animals—Monkey Business

Talkin' English: Going to Movies

Visit us on the Web at
www.TargetsInEnglish.com
Find us on Facebook
www.Facebook.com/TargetsInEnglish

www.ingramcontent.com/pod-product-compliance
Lightning Source LLC
Chambersburg PA
CBHW060812090426
42737CB00002B/42